EIR (ISSN 0273-6314) *is published weekly
(50 issues), by EIR News Service, Inc.,
P.O. Box 17390, Washington, D.C. 20041-0390.
(703) 777-9451 ext. 415*

European Headquarters: E.I.R. GmbH, Postfach
Bahnstrasse 9a, D-65205, Wiesbaden, Germany
Tel: 49-611-73650
Homepage: http://www.eirna.com
e-mail: eirna@eirna.com
Director: Georg Neudecker

Montreal, Canada: 514-461-1557

Denmark: EIR - Danmark, Sankt Knuds Vej 11,
basement left, DK-1903 Frederiksberg, Denmark.
Tel.: +45 35 43 60 40, Fax: +45 35 43 87 57. e-mail:
eirdk@hotmail.com.

Mexico City: EIR, Sor Juana Inés de la Cruz 242-2
Col. Agricultura C.P. 11360
Delegación M. Hidalgo, México D.F.
Tel. (5525) 5318-2301
eirmexico@gmail.com

Seize This Moment

EIR Contents

www.larouchepub.com Volume 43, Number 51, December 16, 2016

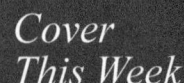

Cover
This Week

Detail from "The Battle of Alexander at Issus" (333 BC), by Albrecht Altdorfer, 1529.

wikipedia

I. Seize This Moment

HELGA ZEPP-LAROUCHE

Donald Trump and the New International Paradigm

This is an edited transcript of a Dec. 12 address by Mrs. Zepp-La-Rouche to a Schiller Institute/EIR seminar in Copenhagen. She was introduced by the Chairman of the Schiller Institute in Denmark, Tom Gillesberg. The audio of Mrs. Zepp-LaRouche's statement is available at https://youtu.be/XWA-6PYhu4SM .

Tom Gillesberg: Introducing Helga is very difficult, because she's simply been involved in so many things over the last half-century that it's almost difficult to describe: One can say that she began her career of the activities she's in right now in 1971, when as a fresh, young journalist, she came to China, and had a chance to see what was then definitely not a developed country. And after she came back home—after going around the world— she joined the LaRouche movement, and then married Lyndon LaRouche and became an international leader in the question of how to create a new paradigm for the world, which would give the whole world a chance for real economic development for a new, just world economic order.

In that process, in 1984 she founded the Schiller Institute. Later, with the fall of the Berlin Wall, she became very active in arranging conferences both in Western and Eastern Europe, and in the United States on using the great potential of that time. Later, when that did not really materialize, she became a driving force in the establishment of the Eurasian Land-Bridge,

Schiller Institute
Helga Zepp-LaRouche addresses the Schiller Institute/EIR seminar in Copenhagen.

and what she described in many conferences in Europe, in China, and other places, as the "New Silk Road" policy for development of the whole world. And as you all know, this is now the policy that the Chinese government is carrying out. And for that reason, I think she is the right person to have here today to discuss all of this in light of the incoming new Presidency in the United States. So, please welcome Helga Zepp-LaRouche. [applause]

Helga Zepp-LaRouche: Good morning ladies and gentlemen. As Tom already noted, we are living in very, very interesting times. This is actually, I think, a Chinese wish, that people say "I wish that you should live in interesting times," and I think we do. Because we are right now in a completely changing strategic situation, which is characterized by completely different vectors of development, and, therefore, it's almost impossible to predict which of these vectors will be the victorious ones. I have an inclination about which one that is going to be, but nothing is in safe areas, nothing is in an area where you could lie back and say "OK this thing is fine," because it's not.

Because you have, I would say, three fundamentally different dynamics. The first one, which concerns us here in Europe, which is the fact that there is, right now, a global revolution against the system of globalization underway. And that is not finished, and it will not stop until the causes for this global revolution are remedied. I think the first massive manifestation was the Brexit

White House Photo by Lawrence Jackson

President Barack Obama, with Secretary of State Hillary Rodham Clinton, Sept. 12, 2012, delivers a statement regarding the attack on the U.S. consulate in Benghazi, Libya.

And, again, many people were in disbelief. And one week later, you had the mortgage crisis in the U.S. breaking out; you had the collapse of this major bridge, which he also had predicted. He said that there will be a collapse of infrastructure, and one week later, the bridge, I think it was in Minnesota, broke down.

A Pregnant Moment

This collapse of globalization, I will talk about in a little while, but it is basically the unifying element between the Brexit, the Trump vote, and now the "No" to the referendum in Italy. Naturally, if you have a system of government where too many people are left behind, where the gap between rich and poor becomes unbearably wide, then eventually such revolts occur. So this is one dynamic, which is obviously affecting the trans-Atlantic sector.

But then you have a more happy dynamic, which is the New Silk Road/Belt and Road initiative initiated by China three years ago, which is already, now, twelve times larger than the Marshall Plan which led to the reconstruction of the postwar Germany and other countries; and it already involves 100 countries and large international institutions. It involves already the majority of mankind, 4.4 billion people, and it is growing very, very rapidly. It has the potential to eventually be the victorious one, because it is based on the idea of "win-win cooperation," where every country can participate, to its own benefit and the benefit of all others.

And then, the newest, third vector of development, which is completely undetermined yet as to where it will go—but nevertheless it is a completely new thing—is the election of Donald Trump to be the next President of the United States.

Up to the present day, the neocon-dominated media in the trans-Atlantic sector are really not grappling with the situation that there is a new U.S. President. They're still in a pre-election mode of unbelievable slanders and spins; as a matter of fact, when the election campaign was underway, I talked with an American who was in the United States, watching Trump's speeches and the reaction of the population. And then he came to Europe and he said, "the media here are portraying this in such a wrong way!" I'm not defending the manners of Mr.

last June in Great Britain, where the majority of the people voted to leave the European Union.

The second major manifestation of this was the rejection of Hillary Clinton, and with that, also a rejection of the policies of the 16-year U.S. Presidencies of Bush and Cheney and Obama, because Obama was really the total continuation of the previous policies of Bush and Cheney. He was not the Messiah who many people believed he would be. But we never thought that. As a matter of fact, I remember that when Obama was speaking in front of 200,000 people in Berlin, I wrote an editorial, "Obama, the Soufflé"—a lot of outside, but not much substance. And I also said at that point, which was not very popular, I said "the Germans apparently always need a leader to follow. Sometimes he is called Adolf, sometimes he is called the Dalai Lama, sometimes he is called Gorby, now he is called Barack." And that was not popular, but we had looked at Obama more closely, and I think we turned out to be right, if you look at the continuation of the wars in the Middle East and the killing policy of the drones, and similar things.

Now, I also want to remind people that my husband, Lyndon LaRouche, made a very famous international webcast on July 25, 2007, which was one week before the secondary mortgage crisis in the United States erupted, where he said, "Globalization is finished. This is the beginning of a global crisis which will not stop."

Trump; do not misunderstand me. The famous German Baron von Knigge, who developed the code of behavior of civilized people, would probably turn in his grave about some of the things Trump does. But, you know, there is a difference between substance and admittedly questionable behavior.

Now, what Trump did, which I think is the most important—the moment he got elected he got on the phone and he talked to Russsian President Putin and Chinese President Xi Jinping, and all sides afterwards confirmed that the intention was to normalize and improve the relationship between the United States and Russia, and the United States and China. And I think this, for any person who is in their right mind, is the most important: Because if Hillary Clinton had been elected, we would be on a short road to a global confrontation, because her plans to establish a no-fly zone over Syria implied the immediate possibility of this conflict going completely out of control and leading to a global confrontation.

So naturally, this is not yet completely remedied. Because it is now Dec. 12th, and it is still five or six weeks until Trump gets into the White House, and you can see very clearly that Obama is trying to create as much chaos on the way out of the White House as he possibly can. He just made a decree where he basically ordered the arming of the rebels in Syria, including providing them with so-called MANPADs, that is shoulder-fired missiles which can shoot down planes; which could really also shoot down American planes, or other planes, so it's a very incredible thing. And I think it's very important that Trump is completely opposed to this. And so is Rep. Tulsi Gabbard, who is a very young, talented congresswoman from Hawaii, who introduced a bill in reaction to this—she's from the Democratic Party—but she introduced a bill prohibiting arms sales to such rebel groups and is leading a bipartisan effort to this effect.

There is also the effort by the neocons to ruin the

U.S. President-elect Donald Trump

relationship with Russia and China in the remaining period as much as possible. For example, the neocon Heritage Foundation in the United States sent a delegation in October to Taiwan. This was Ed Feulner and Stephen Yates, who used to be the national security aide to Dick Cheney, and Reince Priebus, the new member of the Trump team. They went to Taiwan; and this was coordinated with the effort by the Taiwanese government to use the incoming new Presidency to change the "One China" policy. So they had hired three lobbyists: Bob Dole, Richard Gephardt, and Tom Daschle, to get access to the President-elect and get a policy change. And it was that combination of Heritage plus lobbyists, who arranged the phone call of Taiwanese President Tsai with Trump, congratulating Trump for his election. And Trump took the phone call, and this was then made a big affair by the international media, because this violated the One China policy.

Our Active Role

The Chinese government took a very laid-back attitude; they said this was the fault of President Tsai and they didn't blame Trump so much. But obviously, such maneuvers are taking place, but they're probably offset by the fact that Trump appointed the next U.S. Ambassador to China to be Terry Branstad, who is the Governor of Iowa and a personal friend of President Xi Jinping since 1985, when Xi Jinping came to Iowa for the first time to do some agricultural training, deals and so forth. Branstad would in all likelihood be completely opposed to having a trade war with China, or sanctions, and will insist on good relations.

If you look at the other appointments which are known so far in the new Trump team, they're all interesting people, because most of them are explicitly anti-neocon. They're very conservative, but that's not the same thing as neocon, in the same way that the Nazis were not conservatives. There is a difference between such things.

Carnegie Council/youtube screenshot
Lt. Gen. Michael T. Flynn

Office of the President-elect
James Mattis

ExxonMobil
Rex Tillerson

For example, Gen. Michael Flynn, who is now the new National Security Advisor of Trump, was kicked out of the position of Director of the Defense Intelligence Agency in 2014, because he had criticized Obama for arming the different terrorist groups: al-Qaeda, al Nusra—ISIS did not yet exist at that point; but he said that these groups intended to build an Islamic caliphate, and it was the intention of Obama to have them do that, in order to topple the legitimate, elected governments. Which was the truth, and he was kicked out for that reason; so he's now the National Security Advisor of Trump.

Then there is Gen. James Mattis, the retired CENT-COM commander, a four-star general who is known to be completely against the wars for regime-change purposes, as is Flynn and Gen. John Kelly (ret.)—and all of them share the idea that the United States should stop intervening in the affairs of other countries, toppling regimes, and making color revolutions and similar things.

Trump about two weeks ago made a speech in Cincinnati, where he laid out his foreign policy approach. He said we should absolutely not have these foreign wars. We should stop having wars against regimes about which we know nothing, which only leads to chaos, and we should instead build friendship with old friends, and make new friendships.

Another appointment causing a big freakout on the neocon side is that of Rex Tillerson, the head of Exxon-Mobil, who is supposed to become the new Secretary of

State. And he had been given the most important Russian friendship award by President Putin.

It may be there are some other interesting appointments; there are also some problematic appointments, like three or four members of Goldman Sachs who are in the economic team. We have to see how that plays out, because in the worst case it's a continuation of Wall Street policies. In the best case, it's like Franklin D. Roosevelt's appointment of Joe Kennedy, who was a member of the banking lobby, but he got him to implement Glass-Steagall, because, as he said, "it takes one to know one," so you need someone who knows the business. But I don't want to make a prediction on that, because Goldman Sachs is also the origin of European Central Bank (ECB) President Mario Draghi and such people.

Obama is now throwing another hand grenade into the situation, by ordering Director of National Intelligence James Clapper to "investigate" Russia's supposed theft of the U.S. election through cyber attacks against Hillary, the Democratic National Committee, and so forth. This is a big thing; all the papers are saying Russia intervened in the U.S. election. All the German papers are now repeating the same thing, and they're saying, "Oh, we have to be so concerned that Russia will meddle in the upcoming Federal election in Germany next year." But Trump already denounced that, and said this is a big lie—it is the same kind of lie as the "weapons of mass destruction" lie against Iraq. And there was also a hearing in Congress, where the FBI testified that there is absolutely no evidence for Russian involvement in these attacks. Trump said these attacks could have come from anyplace, from New Jersey, or anywhere else.

And also, as the President of South Korea is being impeached, the South Korean Defense Minister announced that the deployment of the THAAD missiles, which are regarded by Russia and China as a strategic threat, is being sped up, which is not a good development at all.

What is the perspective for what we want to do?—because we're not just looking at Trump, analyzing in a contemplative way; but we have a very active approach. We want the United States to join the New Silk Road dynamic. Because if you have recently been in the United States, the United States is in urgent need of infrastructure. If you drive on the highway from Washington to New York, there are potholes which are really so big that you can't drive a small car, because you can just vanish into them. And don't try to go on a fast-train system in the United States, because there is none. Only tiny Amtrak, but it can be as slow as anything.

The Crisis of the System

So we want the United States to have an infrastructure program, which Trump already announced. He said he wants to build an infrastructure program with a $1 trillion investment in the next years and make the infrastructure in the United States the most modern in the world. Now, that's quite a mouthful, because then he has to compete with the Chinese infrastructure program which is unbelievably modern and fast-growing—up to 2014 China has built 20,000 km of fast train systems, and the Chinese fast trains are excellent; they're fast, they're smooth, they're quiet. And by the year 2020 China will have built 50,000 km of fast train systems, connecting every large city in China with such a system. So Trump has quite a lot to do.

But obviously, if this infrastructure program in the United States were connected to the New Silk Road efforts via the Bering Strait and to Latin America, you could have a completely different paradigm in a very short period of time. And one can almost be certain that the new U.S. Ambassador Branstad will advise that the United States join the AIIB, the Asian Infrastructure Investment Bank.

This is very urgent, because the United States is in a terrible crisis. The crisis in the United States is much worse than people in Europe normally know. The National Center for Health Statistics just put out new figures about an increase in the death rate of people in the United States: For example, from 2014-2015, the death rate in the United States went up. That is really unbelievable, because normally in the industrialized world, the death rate would continuously fall! Longevity would increase. But here, from the 10 major diseases, the death rate increased; the average life expectancy for men decreased from 76.5 to 76.3, that is 0.2 year of shrinkage; and for women from 81.3 to 81.2, by 0.1 year. Since life expectancy is the best indicator for the wellbeing of people, this is really unbelievable. And in the 16 years of the Obama and Bush administrations, the suicide rate quadrupled in all age groups, for reasons of drug addiction, alcoholism, depression, especially white women—white women in rural areas.

Obviously, this is the result of globalization, because the Wall Street people became richer and richer, but the so-called rust belt in the United States became poorer—those states which were previously industrialized, which Hillary Clinton was too arrogant to even visit in the election campaign, because she thought she had these states in her pocket—but these were the states that voted against her.

But in Europe the situation is not any better, at least in parts of Europe. As a result of the Troika policy, you have now impoverishment of 45% of the Greek population; 45% of people in Greece are living below the poverty line. That is no good!

In Italy, you have now an unemployment rate, estimated even by the EU Commission, of 23% average, but 50% of the youth—every other youth has no job and no chance to get higher education, which means they have no future. And this is even 65% in Calabria, Sardinia, and Sicily, despite the fact that every year, 100,000 people leave the Mezzogiorno because they have no choice, so there is a tremendous brain drain. And one person in four in Italy is regarded as poor, and the health system has completely collapsed, as it has in Greece.

This is why the people voted "No" to the referendum of Renzi, just a week ago, because what this referendum was supposed to do is to streamline the Italian Constitution according to the guidelines of the European Union, and in that way fulfill the requirements of JP Morgan which had already put out a study some years ago, saying some of these European constitutions should be changed. They were written in the postwar period, and they provide too many protections for labor, and should be rewritten. And that was what Renzi was trying to do, by taking the EU guidelines and changing the Italian Constitution according to these provisions—but the Italian people rejected it, 60-40%, and now Renzi is out. This is a situation which is reflective of the deep-rooted rejection by the population of these policies.

What was the reaction of the European Central Bank to the "No" to the referendum *and* to the Italian banking crisis, which threatened to fully erupt, because if these requirements of the EU could not be fulfilled, then the conflict between the national interests of Italy and the EU would break out even more. What did the ECB do? ECB President Mario Draghi announced that he would continue quantitative easing forever. He said, at least until the end of 2017, I will reduce the quantitative easing from €80 to €60 *billion* per month—that's still a lot of money—but I may increase it even higher than €80 billion if required, and it could even continue beyond 2017. Which means that the total amount of ECB state bond buying is now €2.3 trillion, which is quite amazing.

Now, what that amounts to is that you start to finance the deficit of states with the printing press, and that is exactly what the Reichsbank in Germany did in 1923. And people should not be fooled by the so-called "low inflation" rate, because the Reichsbank financed the war debt and the reparations of Germany for four years before it became visible. But then in spring 1923, it erupted very, very quickly.

Now, this measure by the ECB is so outrageous that even the neoliberal house organ of Frankfurt, Germany's financial capital, the *Frankfurter Allgemeine Zeitung,* had an amazing editorial a week ago, where they said the ECB broke all rules of Maastricht and all the EU treaties; they have now become a debt union, a union of people where everyone has to take care of everyone else's losses; whereas the rules said that this should never happen. It is a violation of the non-assistance clause; and it basically makes the savers poorer, and the speculators richer. And then the editorial says: If the politicians denounce this reaction of the people against this policy as "populism," they are in a complete state of denial.

And that is absolutely true, because there is such a thing as natural law. If you violate the living conditions of people for a very long period of time, they may take it for a while, because people are—you know, sometimes they trust the government, and they think things will not be so bad. But if it removes the basis for existence of ever large numbers of people, then eventually you see exactly what you're seeing right now.

Now, what you have is a complete state of denial of reality, on the side of those people who say "this is just populism, demagogues who hype up the people," and it is interesting that the neoliberal/neocon press, both in the English-speaking world and in Germany, chose the same word as the "word for the year." In English it's "post-truth," and in German it's *postfaktisch*, which is the same thing—which is the idea that people no longer react to the facts, but they only react to feelings—and that the facts are that everybody is better off, but people have a feeling that the are worse off, and therefore they only listen to their feelings, and therefore. . . . You know, it's really a manipulation. So whenever you read this word "post-truth" or *postfaktisch*, I'm sure its one of these creations of psychological think-tanks to manipulate the people. Because I would say that what is at work is not *postfaktisch* or post-truth; what is at work is natural law. That there is a justice in the universe and in the political order, which you cannot violate for a very long period of time. You cannot make the rich, the upper 0.1% and upper 1% of people—you know, 80 people now own as much wealth as 3.5 *billion* people! Now, does that make sense? No! It doesn't make sense, and you cannot have a world where this goes on.

So the rules of the European Union, ECB, all have been broken completely, and there is a legal principle which is called "*Pacta sunt servanda*": "Treaties must be observed." If you don't have that legal principle, there is no order in the world any more; if you can make a pact, a treaty, and then everybody turns around and violates it, you have chaos. And it is really the EU itself dismantling the EU; it's not the people, it's this unjust system which is doing that.

So it is no surprise that this rebellion against the system is taking place, and if you take this word "globalization," another word for the same thing is "Anglo-American empire." Now, Anglo-American empire is really the power of Wall Street and the City of London, and they said up to recently, "we are in a unipolar world; we set the rules." This was the purpose of TTIP for Europe, the trans-Atlantic trade relations; and of TPP for the trans-Pacific trade relations. And Obama had an article in the *Washington Post* several months ago, where he said: The purpose of TPP is that it is the United States that sets the rules in Asia, not China. And he said it as explicitly as that.

But the world is no longer a unipolar world; that's an illusion. And one has to really look at the EU from that standpoint, that since the Maastricht Treaty,... and I just want to remind people that with the unification of Germany, people said, "they have to pay a price, they have to give up the dmark for the euro." It was especially Thatcher, Mitterrand and Bush, who insisted that the price for German reunification would be the euro. And it was an attempt to make the European Union the pro-consul of this Anglo-American empire, the regional stake-holder, so to speak, of this power of Wall Street and the City of London.

Paratroopers on NATO maneuvers in Estonia are part of the largest military mobilization on Russia's western border since World War II.

People have wondered, maybe, why did nobody do anything to correct the casino economy after the crash, the systemic crisis of 2008? One could have thought this was almost a systemic crisis. People were completely freaked out that this could lead to a meltdown, with terrible chaos. But then, they decided to do the same thing, over and over: rather they made it worse. What did they do? They implemented quantitative easing, money printing, negative interest rates, you now have money in most countries, you bring it to the bank and you have to *pay*. No more interest, but you have to pay! And then, they even talk about "helicopter money," that was the old idea of Ben Bernanke. He said, before we would allow a banking crisis to take down the system, we would fly helicopters over the cities and just throw money out, to create as much liquidity as required. And now, the last phase of it is what the ECB is doing to with state financing by the printing press.

That cannot go on. But this is the reason that I'm saying that this revolt will go on until the causes of the injustice are remedied, and we will again have governments which take care of the common good of the people. Now, it is almost the case, that people in Europe, when you say the purpose of government is to be for the common good of the people, they look at you and say, "What?! I never heard such a thing." Because politi-cians are there because they want to have a position, privileges, they want to be reelected ... but to be for the common good of the people? This is almost an exotic idea. [laughter]

So unfortunately, this unipolar world attempt also had a military-security component, and that was the cause for the eastward expansion of the EU and NATO. That is why NATO is continuously moving toward the borders of Russia; the EU in the same way: This is the whole reason for the Ukraine crisis, because the EU wanted to incorporate Ukraine into the EU, which would have had a military component, and that was why all of this Ukraine crisis happened, and not Putin annexing Crimea, which is the official story.

But we saw the encirclement of Russia and China, the building of a global anti-ballistic missile system which was read correctly by the Russian and the Chinese military as an attempt to prepare a first-strike capa-bility with the ability to take out the second strike capa-bility of these countries; where naturally, both Russia and China said we cannot allow that, and we will have to take adequate countermeasures. And that was the road which we were on with Obama. This is why many military experts said that we are in a crisis more danger-ous than at the height of the Cold War; and if you re-member, the height of the Cold War was the Cuban Missile Crisis, which brought us to the brink of extinc-tion. And if people say this was more dangerous, and it really is more dangerous, then people should take this seriously!

And with this "unipolar world" came the idea of regime change against every country that would not submit: This was the reason for the war against Afghanistan, Iraq, Libya, Syria, Ukraine, and the color revolutions; and so if you look now at the result of this, it's a string of one policy failure after another. For example, Chas Freeman, who is a former U.S. ambassador to Saudi Arabia, and other countries, made a very interesting speech about a year ago in Washington, where he said: even if you look at this policy of foreign intervention and wars from a narrow American standpoint, they have not served U.S. interests. U.S. interests and the U.S. reputation in the world have deteriorated; the whole creation of this terrorism is the result of it; the world has become much more insecure as a consequence.

The New Paradigm

Now the really good news is to come to the dynamic I was describing: And that is that the new paradigm of a completely new set of international relations is already fully underway. As I said, it involves the greater part of mankind. When President Xi Jinping announced the New Silk Road/"One Belt, One Road" policy initiative in September 2013 in Kazakhstan, we of the Schiller Institute were naturally *extremely* happy, because those of you who have known us for a longer period of time—and Tom referenced it already—you know that this is what we have been working for, for the last quarter of a century. Because when the Wall came down in Berlin, we were prepared for that, because Mr. LaRouche had already predicted in 1984, that the Soviet Union and the Comecon would collapse if they stuck to their then-existing military policy.

So, in 1988, Mr. LaRouche and I gave a press conference in Berlin, where he said, Germany will be soon unified, and we would develop the East, or the Comecon countries, with modern technologies, starting with Poland. And then, when the Wall came down, within a week, I wrote a leaflet. I said, "Continue, Beloved Germany," and then I said what Germany should do, because we *knew* this would happen. And then we proposed the integration of Eastern and Western Europe through infrastructure corridors; and when the Soviet Union collapsed in '91, we said, okay, we will extend this European program to become a Eurasian program. Let's connect the population and industrial centers of Europe with those of Asia through development corridors, and we called it the Eurasian Land-Bridge, the New Silk Road.

And we held *hundreds* of conferences and seminars all over the world for this perspective, and in 1996, China organized a big conference in Beijing, which they called, on our suggestion, "The Regions along the Eurasian Land-Bridge and Their Development." And at that point China already wanted to have the Eurasian Land-Bridge as the long-term strategic perspective of China.

Then the Asia crisis came in '97 and the whole effort was interrupted. But in 2013, President Xi Jinping put the New Silk Road on the agenda, and ever since, this is developing to be the largest infrastructure and development program ever in history.

It is an unbelievable dynamic, and just because you don't read about it much in the media, it doesn't mean it's not happening. It is very much happening, and the basis of it is that China is exporting the Chinese economic model to all other participating countries. And the Chinese economic model, for anybody who has been in China, is unbelievable. The German economic miracle was also very remarkable, but the Chinese economic miracle is probably even more remarkable, because it's a much larger country involving 1.4 billion people. They just recently published a white paper showing that China has lifted 700 million out of extreme poverty; and by the year 2020, they want to lift the remaining 5.7% of poor people out of this condition, and have no more poverty in China.

So, China, by following the reforms of Deng Xiaoping, and completely reversing the course of the Cultural Revolution, has repeated in 30 years an economic development that the industrialized countries took 200 years or 150 years to achieve. And if you have been in Shanghai or Beijing or Chongqing or Chengdu, or any other large city in China, it is really amazing what a level of development China has accomplished. And now they're exporting that by making the New Silk Road the common motor for development: They're building fast train systems, infrastructure corridors, and energy production and distribution.

They're building science cities with developing countries. Xi Jinping was just in Ecuador, where they're building a science city. President Correa of Ecuador said that China and Ecuador are united in their wish to be at the frontier of science and have the most advanced technologies. Ecuador is still a poor, developing country, but they're now inspired by China to leapfrog,—

Yachay, Ecuador's City of Knowledge, under development with Chinese funding, is intended to serve as a regional hub for a variety of scientific, technological, and trade activities. China views it as a key component of the One Belt, One Road perspective.

Carlos Silva/Vicepresidencia

Students working in the lab at Yachay Technical University.

you know, to not just repeat what the industrial countries were doing over 200 years, but to leapfrog to the top. And China is helping them.

And this has completely changed the dynamic in the whole world. So, this now involves more and more regions of the world. The original route goes from China through Central Asia to Europe; but now it is already spreading to the ASEAN countries, and to the 16 + 1 Central and East European Countries (CEEC), who are all happy when China comes and invests in infrastructure in a railway between Serbia and Hungary and Poland. Even Poland—Nursultan Nazarbayev, the President of Kazakhstan, was recently at a conference in Poland, where he said that they are now building a development corridor from Kazakhstan to Poland, through Russia, and that he personally wants to help to overcome the tensions between Poland and Russia.

The Peace Order of the 21st Century

So what we are looking at is not just economic development, but this is the basis of a peace order for the 21st century: Because if you have common develop-

ment for everybody, then you also tend to eliminate the causes for war. It also involves more and more Latin American countries. In the recent trip of Xi Jinping to Latin America, he visited Ecuador, Peru, and Chile; and China is now building a transcontinental railway from Brazil to Peru, several tunnels between Chile and Argentina, a new canal in Nicaragua, and other such things.

Now the process of economic integration is going extremely rapidly. At the Vladivostok Economic Forum in the beginning of September, there was not only the integration of the Eurasian Economic Union with the "One Belt, One Road" policy, but also Japanese Prime Minister Shinzo Abe was there. And Japan is now massively investing in the Far East of Russia. Then, this integration was continued at the G20 summit in Hangzhou, where China said the new economic philosophy will be innovation. Only through innovation will we get out of the economic crisis. And it was continued at the ASEAN summit and the East Asia summit in Laos; at the BRICS conference in Goa, India, in October; and at the recent APEC summit in Lima, Peru in November.

Now, China and the other Asian countries, and the BRICS countries have also constructed a lot of new banks: The AIIB, the Asian Infrastructure Investment Bank; the New Development Bank; the Silk Road Fund, the Maritime Silk Road Fund, and other banks like the Shanghai Cooperation Organization bank, and the South Bank of the South Asian countries. And all of these banks are built on a completely different principle than the IMF and the World Bank, because these new banks are only there for infrastructure and other investment in the real economy, not for speculation. And this is very, very important, because it is almost like the lifeboat for the sinking *Titanic* of the collapsing trans-Atlantic financial system, because it is a model of what banking should be. You don't need speculation; you don't need derivatives; you don't need all of this; but what these banks deliberately intend to do, is to take care of the deficit of infrastructure investment on the part of the IMF and the World Bank for the last decades.

The condition of the Third World, of Africa, and of many Asian and Latin American countries is not natural! If the IMF and the World Bank had done for the last 50 years what these new Asian banks are doing now, you wouldn't have poverty! You would have blooming gardens! There is no *need* to have such destruction as we are seeing in many parts of the world, except that it was the intention to keep these countries down, and to introduce this whole idiotic idea of limits to growth, resource exploitation, and all the rest.

So these new banks are there, and you can see, with Trump's announcement that he will build a trillion-dollar infrastructure program, that the world could really grow together! The chairwoman of the Foreign Affairs Committee of the Chinese National People's Congress, Mme. Fu Ying, was recently in New York, and gave a speech in which she said: The infrastructure program of Trump can be the bridge to the "One Belt, One Road." And that is exactly what we in the Schiller Institute said in a study in 2014, which you can see at the book table: "The New Silk Road Becomes the World Land-Bridge." We had one chapter which we added later on, on building U.S. infrastructure in connection with the rest of world development.

And at a recent intervention in New York, one of our colleagues intervened in a presentation with Henry Kissinger. And he asked, "Mr. Kissinger, what do you think about the LaRouche proposal and the Chinese proposal to have the United States join the One Belt, One Road?" You should know that the relations between my husband and Kissinger over the decades were not the most amiable, because he criticized many of Kissinger's policies. So, it was quite amazing that he said: "Yes, the One Belt, One Road is very important

en.people.cn

The just-completed Addis-Djibouti Railway, constructed using Chinese design, equipment, and operations, is said to shrink the trip between Addis Ababa and Djibouti on the Red Sea from one week to ten hours.

for the world." And Kissinger is meeting with Trump regularly now, and obviously you remember that Kissinger was the one who came to China in 1971 to prepare the visit of Nixon. It was just while I was in China that Kissinger came. And this was a big thing! Because up to that point, the Chinese outlook was that the United States was a paper tiger which can easily be defeated in the conflict with Vietnam and so forth. So to invite Kissinger and then Nixon was a real dramatic change in Chinese policy—so it is quite interesting that Kissinger would say this now.

LaRouche's Four Laws

Now, obviously, infrastructure in the United States is not the only problem, because you need to stop the casino economy, the Wall Street excesses which have led to this crisis. But Trump in the election campaign promised repeatedly that he would introduce Glass-Steagall, the banking separation law of Franklin D. Roosevelt. Now we have to see if he will do it. There is now a lot of expectation; some of the progressive Democrats have said that they will collaborate with Trump on this point, but we have to see.

And again, we are not looking at him passively, but we are taking an active attitude, we are talking with Congressmen and with Senators, and we are bringing activists to meet with them from the different states. But the purpose is that we need the full package of solutions that have been proposed by Mr. LaRouche, who designed the four fundamental laws which are necessary to remedy this crisis. And the first of these laws is the implementation of Glass-Steagall. We have to do exactly what Roosevelt did in 1933: You separate the banks. The commercial banks will get protected. The investment banks must take care of themselves, without taxpayer money, without quantitative easing—and if they turn out to have red figures in their books, they have to close down. That's simply what should happen, and we really don't need them.

But that is only the first step. Then you go to national banking; this is not some socialist or communist idea, but it is what the first Treasury Secretary of the United States Alexander Hamilton did, who really united the United States by taking the debt from the War of Independence, by unifying the states' debts and making them into a Federal debt, and then implemented taxation to stabilize the debt, and use that as a basis for new credits for investment.

Now, that model has been repeated. It was done by John Quincy Adams, who created the Second Bank of the United States, from 1816 to 1836; and this First and Second Bank of the United States were both used only for investment in the real economy. And it was implemented again in principle by Lincoln, who was advised by Henry C. Carey, and went to the Greenback system, to U.S. notes.

This system, by the way, in which Lincoln was advised by Henry C. Carey, was also the means through which Germany transformed itself in a few years, from a feudal country into an industrialized country at the time of Bismarck. This is very important: Because if you read all the biographies of Bismarck, you will not find one reference to Henry C. Carey. And you will not find a reference to Wilhelm von Kardorff. If anyone wants to study this period in more depth, I can only advise him to read a little booklet called "Against the Stream," where Wilhelm von Kardorff, who was the head of the German industry association at the time of Bismarck, explained the physical-economic reasoning

Henry C. Carey

Wilhelm von Kardorff

which was what persuaded Bismarck to abandon free trade, and go to a protectionist system like what Lincoln had done in the United States.

It was the same system which was implemented by Franklin D. Roosevelt as the Reconstruction Finance Corporation, which gave the credits for the New Deal, for all the infrastructure projects, the Tennessee Valley Authority project, the Rural Electrification, and the CCC program. They pulled youth into real education and jobs programs, and that was the way the United States was led by Roosevelt out of the Depression, and became the most industrialized, developed country by the end of the Second World War. And it was that same approach which the German Kreditanstalt für Wiederaufbau, the Credit Bank for Reconstruction, used to achieve the German Economic Miracle in the postwar period, because the KfW was based on the Reconstruction Finance Corporation of Roosevelt.

The purpose of this credit system is not just simple investment, but the purpose must be to increase the productivity of the production process through the injection of science and technology, and to go to higher forms of energy flux density associated with these higher technologies. It must also be capital-intensive.

But the fourth law of Mr. LaRouche is really almost the most important, because if you look at the effects of the globalization of the last five decades, since approximately the death of Kennedy, they have destroyed much of the productive capacity needed to maintain the existing world population of 7 billion people. This has been because of a lot of wrong economic principles, like

The Experimental Advanced Superconducting Tokamak at China's Institute of Plasma Physics, in Hefei.

tech.sina.com.cn

cheap labor, "buy cheap, sell dear," and "control the trade." In the beginning phase even China was a cheap-labor country. The actual productive powers of the trans-Atlantic world have collapsed.

So this is why Africa is poor; this is why the Middle East is poor; why many other countries are still poor. So you need to have an injection of science and technology, to increase the productivity of the entire capacities worldwide, and the only efficient way, the necessary way must be a crash program for the development of thermonuclear fusion power and space technology.

Because these are the areas which you can say with absolute scientific certainty, will lead to the desired increase in productivity. Now the reason for fusion power is very obvious, because once you have thermonuclear fusion, you will have through the incredibly high heat associated with fusion (100 million degrees), a side technology which is called the fusion torch; and with that you can take all the waste and separate it into different isotopes, and create new raw materials.

So already with deuterium and tritium, which are the fuel for the first generation of fusion power, we will have energy security for all of mankind, and we will have raw materials security, and that is an extremely important goal to reach. But the main reason that we don't have fusion power yet, is because—and we did a thorough investigation of this—if you look at the in-

vestment into fusion in Europe and in the United States, it was always below the threshold needed to make a breakthrough. It was just enough to keep the technology and research going, but if you don't launch the crash program, you will never actually achieve it.

And China—what a surprise—is now the only country which is increasing its investment into fusion research. It made a major breakthrough just recently in the EAST program—Experimental Advanced Superconducting Tokamak—which is in the Institute for Plasma Physics in Hefei, where they were able to stabilize a hydrogen plasma for 100 seconds, and reach a temperature within the plasma of 50 million degrees, which is about half what is needed to keep the fusion process going on the basis of deuterium and tritium.

China has a very ambitious program. It wants to have the first test fusion reactor operating by 2025, producing 200 MW of electricity, and then move immediately to upgrade that into an operating reactor producing 1 GW. But China is already looking at the second generation of fusion power, while they are building the basis for the first generation—and that is immediately associated with the Chinese space program. Next year, in 2017, the Chang'e-5 mission will go to the Moon, where it will land a vehicle—a rover—on the Moon to take samples from the surface and bring them back to Earth.

The Extraterrestrial Imperative

And then, one year later, in 2018, the Chang'e-4 mission is supposed to land a space vehicle for the first time on the far side of the Moon. Now this is very, very exciting, because the far side of the Moon is not disturbed by the radiation coming from the Earth, and therefore on the one hand, you can use it to set up radio-telescopes which you could not use on the near side of the Moon; and this will allow you to have much, much deeper perspectives into the Solar System and the Galaxy and beyond; but you can also start looking at mining helium-3 from the far side of the Moon.

Helium-3 is an isotope of helium, and it is a perfect fuel for the second generation of thermonuclear fusion power, because it allows you to take electricity directly from the physical fusion process for the first time, and not to have to go through turbines or other heat-powered machines.

Now, there are only 15 tons of helium-3 on the Earth; but there are 1-5 million tons on the Moon. And for practically indefinite energy security on the Earth, we only need about 100 tons. So it's important that people understand that we are on the verge of a *completely* new way of organizing affairs on the Earth; and this has everything to do with the long-term ability of mankind to survive as a species.

Mr. LaRouche has developed the correlation of energy-flux density with relative population density. In other words, there is a correlation between the energy density you use in the production process, and the number of people you can maintain. Which is why the idea of "decarbonization" of the world economy is really genocide: Because if you eliminate coal, gas, fossil fuels, nuclear energy, and go only to "alternative" energies, as some people are proposing these days, the population potential you can maintain with that is about 1 billion or less. And that should be very, very clear.

The late German space researcher and rocket scientist Krafft Ehricke is very, very important, and we are planning to have two big conferences next year on the 100th anniversary of his birth: Because he had a vision of why man must go into space.

First of all, he had a very fascinating idea of the evolution of life on the planet. He had the idea that life developed out of the oceans, and then, through photosynthesis, on the land. Then higher species developed, where each species had what we would call nowadays, a higher energy-flux density in its metabolism, and eventually man appeared. And then, man first settled at the rivers and on ocean shores; and then man—because man is the one species which has the creative ability to come up with new technologies all the time—brought infrastructure inland, building roads, waterways, canals, then trains, and in that way started to conquer more and more of the landlocked areas of the continents.

And now, look in that light at the present program of the New Silk Road and our more advanced conception

Krafft Ehricke

of "the New Silk Road must become the World Land-Bridge"; look at this World Land-Bridge report, or this World Land-Bridge idea, which is the conception that you will bring infrastructure development to all landlocked areas in all continents. So with that the infrastructure development of the planet is completed, at least in principle.

And then, the next level, the next stage of infrastructure development is the colonization of nearby space: going to the Moon, industrializing the Moon, and taking the Moon as the starting point for space travel to other heavenly bodies, like Mars and other planets.

So Krafft Ehricke developed something which he called the "the three fundamental laws of astronautics," which I want to read to you, because I think they're extremely important. The first law says:

"1. Nobody and nothing under the natural laws of this universe impose any limitations on man, except man himself"; which is a fundamental idea which used to be normal in European humanism. That man is infinitely perfectable and nothing blocks the perfection of man other than man himself. I think this is an idea which has been almost lost nowadays, because people have become adjusted to the fallacy that everything is limited, everything is known already, and we can't even make fundamental breakthroughs any more—but not so.

And the second law, Krafft Ehricke developed is:

"2. Not only the Earth, but the entire solar system, and as much of the universe as he can reach under the

All China Women's Federation

China expects to complete the construction of its space station, depicted here, by 2023.

species are not Earth-bound, that we are capable of leaving the Earth, and you can already see the next platforms; Mr. LaRouche defined this notion as an economic platform, to specify that the most advanced technology at each level defines a platform. So we had the platform of hunters and gatherers; we had the platform of agriculture; we have the platform of the steam engine, the platform of, let's say, air travel, and the first platform of space activity is the ability of man to even leave the surface of the Earth.

It may not be self-evident that man would get the idea you don't have to stay on the Earth, but that you can develop spacecraft and get into an orbit! Which is about the platform we are now at with the International Space Station (ISS), and with the first Moon landings. And then the second platform will be space travel, where we use installations on the Moon, we industrialize the Moon, we create Moon villages, to then travel from one heavenly body to the next, like from the Moon to Mars.

And then the third level will be that we produce in space what we need, in other words, we don't take food and fuel and other things up in a spacecraft, but that we take the resources existing in space to produce which will be necessary—if we have long-term space travel with spacecraft fueled by fusion energy, for example, which makes it much faster. But you can already see that that will be the next level.

Krafft Ehricke called this process of space travel, "the extraterrestrial imperative of man." This is very beautiful because it implies that once man becomes a space-faring species, that you have to be rational. You cannot go to the Moon and have a fit; it's not good for your health if you do that! So it requires that man become adult, and that man continuously develop new horizons. And I think that's a very beautiful idea.

It is interesting that despite all the greenie ideology which has infested people's minds in the last 40 years,

laws of nature, are man's rightful field of activity." Now that is an equally beautiful idea, that the universe is our garden. It's not just the Earth, but the entire Solar System and whatever else we can reach.

And then in the third law, he says:

"3. By expanding through the universe, man fulfills his destiny as an element of life, endowed with the power of reason and the wisdom of the moral law within himself." That is a very beautiful idea also, that it's our destiny to fill the universe, not only that we have to plant the Earth, as it's said in the Bible, that man has to subdue the Earth and multiply; but that we have to extend ourselves in the universe, because we have the gift of the power of reason, and we have a moral law inside ourselves. That also has been forgotten, that people have an "inner voice," something like a conscience, and that that conscience can be the guideline; many people have forgotten that such a thing exists.

Obviously the significance of this philosophical and also practical dimension of space, is that we as a human that ESA, the European Space Agency, just had a conference with the ministers of the 22 participating countries, and in this context, it took a public opinion poll, and it turned out that 88% of all the people polled were in favor of space exploration: which means they're culturally optimistic concerning the idea of space. And even more, 96% thought that space research gives mankind more opportunities than anything we can do on Earth. For instance, space medicine is the most advanced medicine, and things like that.

Dialog of Classical Cultures

This is very beautiful, because when you are talking about a new paradigm, we want everyone to think like astronauts, cosmonauts, and taikonauts, because all of them, when they come back from the ISS and speak at press conferences, they all say: When you look at Earth from space, you have a completely different perspective. You see one humanity sitting on a small, fragile, blue planet. You don't see borders, you don't see wars, but you see the one mankind—and that is the view which we have to induce people to have if the new paradigm is going to succeed. It is what Xi Jinping calls "a community of destiny for the future of mankind." We are a community of destiny because in former times, civilizations could go under and others could rise at the same time, and neither would know about it. But because of nuclear weapons, the speed of air travel, the possibility of epidemics travelling around the world, and many other factors, we are so much sitting in one boat, that you cannot have one part of the world go under and another one prosper—but we have to really make the jump away from geopolitics to the idea that we are one humanity: And that has to start in the head.

I mean, there will be still legitimate room for nations, for languages, for culture, but you have to start in your mind with the one humanity, and there must never again be an interest of one nation or a group of nations, which is in violation of the interests of mankind as a whole. And either we make that jump or we will not

Nicholas of Cusa, 1401-1461

exist. And I think with the "win-win" perspective of China, and the New Silk Road, we have a realistic possibility of making exactly that jump.

Now we also have to re-establish international law, which has been completely trampled upon by the neocons, which essentially is what's in the UN Charter, which means a total respect for the sovereignty of countries, noninterference in their internal affairs; respect for their different social models; all of this "democracy" and "human rights" was only a pretext anyway, and it should be put in the garbage can. Because you don't have democracy; if Wall Street can buy a Senator for $5 billion you don't have democracy. And I could say a lot about European parties as well.

So, we have to have a new paradigm, and this new paradigm was already envisaged by Nicholas of Cusa in the 15th century, when he said, the only reason that different cultures can communicate with each other is because all of them produce wise people, artists, musicians, and scientists who all speak a universal language. You can have musicians from all nations play in one orchestra, totally understanding each other, because music is a universal language. A scientist who makes a discovery in one country can replicate that discovery in another country, because it's a universal language.

So we have to have a communication on that level, of scientists, of artists, and then there will be no problem among the cultures, and we will have what Nicholas of Cusa also envisioned: a harmony in the universe, because all microcosms develop into a harmonious macrocosm. And that is also the idea of Confucius, who had exactly that same idea of a harmonious development: If all develop their potentialities you will have harmony in the large, and it will also mean the fulfillment of Leibniz's vision that China and Europe reach out and grasp each other's hands, and develop the rest of the world between them and beyond them; and this development will not just be static development, but like a contrapuntal fugue, where the development of each reaches into the other and leads to a beautiful totality.

Now, practically, that means we have to have a Marshall Plan Silk Road program for the reconstruction of the Middle East; now that there is hope for the war to come to an end in Syria, we must bring the reconstruction of all of these countries onto the table. Xi Jinping already said, the Silk Road can be extended into the Middle East. General Flynn, already in 2015, talked about a Marshall Plan for the Middle East. The Chinese don't so much like the term "Marshall Plan" because it has a Cold War connotation, so let's just call it a "New Silk Road Marshall Plan without Cold War connotation"—or whatever. [laughter]

Then, naturally, we also need the participation in that from all the neighboring countries: Russia, China, India, Iran, Italy, France, Germany, Denmark, and the United States, should all work together to rebuild this region! We let it happen when this incredible destruction occurred. I mean, if we didn't cause it, we didn't do anything to stop it, so we have a moral obligation to rebuild this area. And the same goes for the development of Africa.

Xi Jinping already said at the G20 meeting that China will be instrumental in helping to industrialize Africa. And we held a meeting of African representatives in Hamburg, just two weeks ago, where the mood had completely shifted: Different African speakers said: Yes! There is a new paradigm shaping the world. China, India, and Japan are coming to Africa and investing in real things, in bridges and railways—and the Europeans will be sidelined, because they only come with speeches, Sunday sermons, democracy demands, and obligations to pay debt—but they will be left behind if they don't change.

They should come and participate, you know; but it needs our intervention to accomplish exactly that.

So these changes are the key challenge for the next couple of months, because Trump has promised he would get these changes under way in the first hundred days of his Presidency. And we all have to participate in building a completely new set of relations among nations. We have to overcome geopolitics, and build exactly this common community for the future of mankind. We have to realize this program, the New Silk Road must become the World Land-Bridge. And I only want to add one thing, which is very, very important: That together with this economic development,

we must have a new Renaissance of Classical culture; because with globalization you not only had all of these things I described, but you also had a terrible cultural degeneracy. And if you look at the youth culture of today in particular, it is ugly, it is sometimes even Satanic, and you don't need to go to black gothic, you can stay with Madonna to come to the Satanic, and that is obviously the complete destruction of creativity. Note also the fact that Trump has now appointed several people who are known to be hardliners against drugs, like for example, Senator Jeff Sessions, who will be the Attorney General, and others. You know that the drug epidemic is one of the causes for the suicide rate in the United States, and the fact that during the time NATO was in Afghanistan, the drug production there increased forty-fold! Obviously, it was with the permission of the NATO people who were there, because otherwise it wouldn't have happened. This is regarded by Russia, for example, as one of the largest threats to its national security, because 100,000 people per year are affected and many of them die. And therefore, this drug epidemic must be overcome.

But we have to have a beautiful culture and revive the Classical traditions of each nation, and we have heard from Feride Istogu Gillesberg one very beautiful example. I'm absolutely certain that when people come to know the beautiful examples of the other cultures, they will fall in love, and all xenophobia will vanish, and all hatred against foreigners will disappear. Because when they see the best expressions of the culture, of the high point of the other culture, they will realize that the universe is all the more beautiful because there are so many cultures and so many nations. And the world would be much poorer and much more boring if there were only one unipolar culture!

So we should add to this perspective the idea of a dialogue of cultures on the highest level.

And I think we should be very happy, because if this all goes in the right direction, which it is in large part, our subjective obligation to help—and I'm asking all of you to not be passive observers, but to join with the Schiller Institute to help to implement these visions and these ideas—because then, we will be very lucky that we in our lifetime, can live the new paradigm. And the new paradigm will be the first time that man's dignity will be realized—and I think that is a very, very important mission we should all adopt. [applause]

II. World Land-Bridge: The New Apollo Project for Mankind

DR. PATRICK HO

China's Belt and Road Initiative

Here is a transcript of Dr. Ho's address to the Dec. 10, 2016 Schiller Institute conference in New York. His presentation (available here, along with that of Helga Zepp-LaRouche) was centered around a very comprehensive PowerPoint presentation, which is only reproduced in small part here.

Dennis Speed: The world now stands on the threshold of its greatest prospect for progress ever. The continent-size nations, China, India, Russia, and the United States, must work together for this end. China, the world's most powerful economy and the nation with the most advanced orientation to space exploration, is offering to work closely with the United States, which used to have the world's most powerful economy, and the world's most advanced space program. Changes now occurring in the United States, including in its Presidency, make this possible. Just this past week, an indirect exchange between economist Lyndon LaRouche and former Secretary of State Henry Kissinger, regarding China's One Belt, One Road policy, acknowledged that the United States can and should cooperate with the Chinese in this new direction for the world. We can see a return by the United States to Alexander Hamilton's economics, promoting the development of the productive powers of labor, and not the mere harvesting of so-called "natural resources." Human creativity is the only true source of wealth for mankind.

EIRNS

Patrick Ho

The One Belt, One Road policy that has been pursued by the Chinese government, particularly since September 2013, and that government's collaboration with Russia, India, and well over 70 nations worldwide, has always been advocated by the Schiller Institute. The founder of the Schiller Institute, Helga LaRouche, has been known as the "Silk Road Lady" since she spoke at a conference in Beijing in June of 1996. She will be speaking with us a bit later.

In January 1997, 20 years ago, *Executive Intelligence Review* published the report, *The Eurasian Land-Bridge: The New Silk Road—The Locomotive for Worldwide Development.* In November 2014, a new report, *The New Silk Road Becomes the World Land-Bridge*, was released. Two days ago, I received a gift from our first speaker. It's called *The 'Belt and Road' Monograph, 2016*; it is published by the China Energy Fund Committee. This beautiful 111-page report was edited by him and he wrote the preface, entitled, "One Belt, One Road, a New Model of Inclusive Economic Growth and Sustainable Development."

It is my honor to present to you Dr. Patrick Ho, violinist, eye surgeon, and international activist of the China Energy Fund Committee.

Dr. Patrick Ho: Thank you Dennis for a very generous introduction, and I feel very humble. I'm Patrick Ho. I'm sorry, I don't have my bios on me, but you can Google me, just go on to Google and see all my previous lives.

Right now in this fourth reincarnation, the first incarnation, I was a concert violinist. I was a musician. I came to the United States on a music scholarship and stayed for 16 years in the United States. But then after a while I got bored with music, so I pursued other things. Music gives me beauty, but I need something more; I need truth, so I pursued science. And I became a doctor. I graduated with an MD degree from Vanderbilt University in Nashville, Tennessee. And I became an eye surgeon, trained in Boston, at the Massachusetts Eye and Ear Infirmary, and afterwards I went back to Hong Kong and took up the chair as a Professor of Ophthalmology in the Chinese University of Hong Kong in 1984, a position I occupied until 1994, for ten years.

Then, I got bored with surgery, doing the same thing day in and day out. After you do 5,000 cases of retinal detachment surgery, it's not challenging any more. So, I wanted to do something better, I wanted to do something that's *faster* and more *immediate*, that can bring sight, vision, and happiness to people. And being a doctor, I only have two hands. I can operate day in and day out until my face turns blue, and I will still be treating a dozen people.

So I took to teaching, thinking I can teach more people to do that, but then I realized that took many years for them to reach a mature stage to be able to perform the type of surgery that I was performing. So, too slow.

So the fastest way to really bring changes in this society, is through politics, public policy. So I opted for politics. At that time, Hong Kong was undergoing a change, of switching of sovereignty back to Hong Kong, in 1997. So, one thing led to another, I was called upon to join the cabinet in the Hong Kong government, and I was the Home Secretary for the first two terms. The home secretary in Hong Kong is equivalent to a home secretary here, too: Internal affairs, domestic affairs, except for foreign relationships and financial matters, I took care of everything that happened in Hong Kong.

Then I got fed up with politics, because I cannot do

the right thing and lie at the same time. [laughter] And so, retired from the cabinet, I was trying to do something that I had not done before, but I had not decided what I wanted to do when I grow up. [laughter] But finally I was called by Beijing to organize this China Energy Fund Committee, which was very well supported, and it was registered in Hong Kong as a nonprofit think tank, a charitable organization. It's devoted to doing research works and issues related to energy diplomacy, energy strategy, and energy safety.

We chose energy, because if we talk politics, people get very tense and defensive. But if we have a medium of something like energy, it's easier to engage people. But energy to us, is taken in its broadest sense: Energy is anything that propels human civilization to progress, anything that drives society to advances in energy. So it's not only fuel, renewable energy, and fossil fuel energy. It also pertains to spiritual energy, cultural energy, and community energy as well. So, in Chinese this is *néngyuán*, it's a broad word. *Néngyuán.* And we are given a special consultative status by the United Nations Economic and Social Council since 2011. and I've been working very closely with the United Nations, and that's what brought me to New York City almost every other month, or every three months, because we have a lot of things going on with United Nations. We are also registered in the United States, in Arlington, Virginia; we are a 501(c)3 organization. So in a nutshell, that's what we do.

I. A China Story: The Beginning

I brought only about 10 copies of the monograph, because they're very heavy to travel with, and it costs a lot to mail. And I donated ten copies to the Schiller Institute, and those of you who do not have a chance to read a copy of them, you can go to this link and you can download the pdf copy of that free of charge. But we would be very gratified if you could make some donation to our 501(c)3 organization.

Towering over the East of the world for 5,000 years

has been a unique and time-honored ancient civilization with a continuous history and culture—China.

I was very grateful to Bill Jones who attended one of our Belt and Road Forum events last week in Washington. After that we had a very friendly chat, and when he realized I was spending this week in New York City, and one thing led to the other, he got me in touch with Dennis, so I was invited to speak to you this afternoon on One Belt, One Road.

One Belt, One Road is a hot topic. Everyone wants to know a lot more about it. But One Belt, One Road is something that's very Chinese and to understand One Belt, One Road is to understand the "Chineseness," what becomes Chinese, what it takes to be China. So one cannot just talk about One Belt, One Road totally separate from Chinese history and Chinese culture, and actually, in order to really understand China, you have to be a Chinese.

Who said that? John Fairbanks. John Fairbanks— that's what he said! He wrote it in his book, too: The only way to understand China is to become Chinese, to get into the Chinese mind. But you're born what you are, how can you understand Chinese? But what he really meant is: To be Chinese is to understand and appreciate the history and the cultural legacy of China. And if you do that, you understand how the whole thing comes about, in other words, the legacy of what it really takes to become a Chinese.

It's not a face, it's not the color of the skin, it's not the language that you speak: It's the perspective of the world. It's the Chinese outlook on the universe, on various things, on values, on culture, and on heritage.

So to begin with, before I touch on the topic of One Belt, One Road, I will give you a 20 minute capsulated—OK, digested version of "A China Story."

Towering over the East of the world for 5,000 years has been a unique and time-honored, ancient civilization with a continuous history and culture: China.

The industrious and brave Chinese people have made contributions such as the compass, papermaking, gunpowder, and printing to the development and progress of human civilization.

In those five millennia, the Chinese have recorded at least four periods of prosperity.

The first was in the Zhou Dynasty (B.C. 1042-996) in which the Chinese feudal system of administration was introduced.

The second was in the Han Dynasty (B.C. 180-141) when Emperors governed with non-interference, farm-

A China Story

Time-Honored 5,000-Year Ancient Civilization

The Four Great Inventions

CHINA

Compass
Papermaking
Gunpowder
Printing

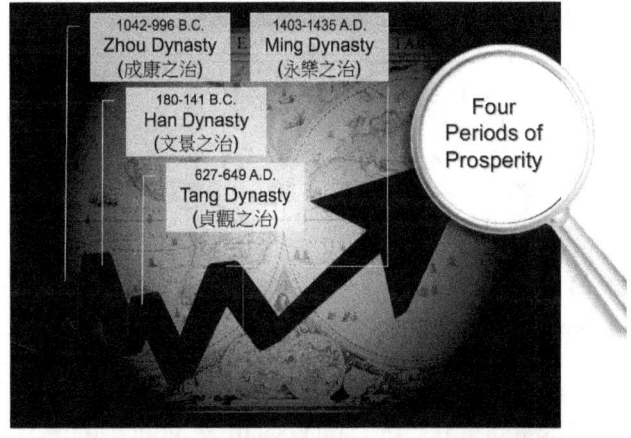

1042-996 B.C.
Zhou Dynasty
(成康之治)

1403-1435 A.D.
Ming Dynasty
(永樂之治)

180-141 B.C.
Han Dynasty
(文景之治)

627-649 A.D.
Tang Dynasty
(貞觀之治)

Four
Periods of
Prosperity

Peace Loving

"I came, I saw, I conquered"
-- Julius Caesar

"I came, I saw, I made friends, and I went home"
-- Zheng He

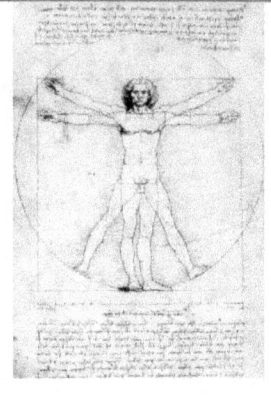

ing, peaceful development, and dispatched envoys to forge the first contacts with the West, opening up the Silk Road for trade.

The third was in the Tang Dynasty (A.D. 627-649) when China's GDP was about one-third of the world's, and students came from Japan and neighboring countries to study in China.

The fourth rise of China occurred in the Ming Dy-

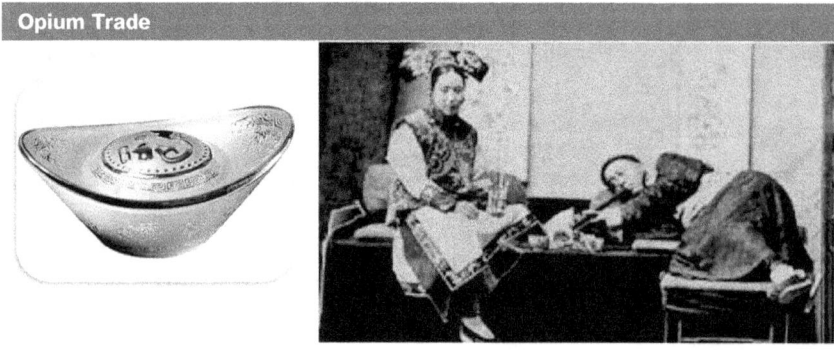

nasty (A.D. 1403-1435) when Admiral Zheng He and his powerful fleets were sent to sail from the South China Sea to the Indian Ocean, to Africa and, arguably, even to America, some 71 years before Columbus.

On the contrary, when the West came to China in the 18th Century to "open it up for trade" at gun-point, the peace-loving Chinese suffered almost ceaseless humiliation from foreign invaders for two centuries.

The Chinese people are a peace loving people. Whereas Julius Caesar said "I came, I saw, I conquered," the Chinese said "I came, I saw, I made friends, and I went home." [laughter]

Not one battle was fought, not one colony seized, and nobody was enslaved. On the contrary, when the West came to China in the 18th Century, to open it up for trade at gunpoint, the peace-loving Chinese suffered almost ceaseless humiliation from foreign invaders for two centuries.

In the 14th Century, the Renaissance delivered Europe from the darkness of the Middle Ages, freed minds, stimulated innovation and creativity in literature, art, science and technology, and hastened the birth of individualism, capitalism, and colonialism.

At the end of the 15th Century, European voyagers set out across the oceans to discover and conquer what lay beyond while colonizing whatever they discovered.

In the later period of the 18th century, Britain's Industrial Revolution, America's War of Independence and the French Revolution dramatically changed the progress of human civilization. Modernization of human society became an unstoppable historical trend, but the Chinese—still complacent at the time with national peace and splendor—were completely unaware of the misfortune about to befall them. Western countries, aiming to enrich themselves with natural resources through their military supremacy, forcibly expanded colonialism to the East. A turbulent situation unimagined ever before, and the most painful period in its history, was about to be forced upon this nation of peace-lovers.

For a long time, China's foreign trade had focused on exporting tea and agricultural products, fine silks and porcelain, which the West purchased with silver dollars. Following the Industrial Revolution and the booming productivity it brought, Britain's most urgent desire was to enlarge its global markets—and, in particular, find a way of getting back the huge amounts it had paid China in silver dollars. British colonists flooded China with opium and so were able to plunder over one and half million kilograms of silver dollars in the following four decades.

In response, and painfully aware of the hazards of opium, the Chinese Government decided to prohibit opium smoking, forced the Western merchants to surrender their stocks of the drug, and destroyed it. In 1840, the opium merchants, nearly all British, together with the British men-of-war, invaded China and launched the First Opium War. China then, as the main power in the East, enjoyed about one-third of global GDP, and had military forces of 800,000. The British had just 7,000 men in their expeditionary force, and fewer than 20,000 at the end of the war. *Yet China lost the war.* Hardly had the Qing government negotiated grossly unequal treaties with Britain and the other invaders when the Second Opium War broke out in 1860. By then China's GDP was 1.6 times that of Britain. *Yet China lost again.*

So as you can see, having a big GDP does not mean anything! You can still lose any war. So a big GDP is *nothing*. So everybody said, China's big GDP is going to save us. No! Big GDP meaning, a big country, doesn't mean a *strong country*. A big GDP is a big country; a strong GDP means military supremacy. But the great country comes from its attractiveness, comes from its soft power, it comes from its cultural legacy.

Accordingly, the Chinese Emperor in 1860 ordered that the advanced technologies of the West must be learned. They must catch up.

The first Westernization Movement saw

First Opium War (1840) Second Opium War (1860)

the initiation of new industries to improve military hardware. New naval and land forces were established. More schools were built and the students were sent overseas for higher education.

The disastrous Sino-Japanese War broke out in 1894

Westernization Movement

The Sino-Japanese War (1894)

The Revolution of 1911

China Joins WWI (1917)

KMT-CPC Rupture (1927)

when China's GDP was *five* times that of Japan. China's newly equipped forces *lost once again*, to Japan.

The Westernization Movement was deficient because China's GDP represented prosperity, but not proportionate national strength. In 1895, a batch of scholars attempted to organize a coup to install a constitutional monarchy; but this Hundred Days' Reform was terminated forcefully 103 days later by the court.

A battle cry became louder in China in the beginning of the 20th century—revolution—with Dr. Sun Yat-sen in the forefront. The revolution broke out in China in 1911 and took down the Qing Dynasty, ending 2,000 years of feudal monarchies, and replacing it with the first Chinese Republic.

The emperor was gone and the pig-tail braid was cut. The Congress, the Provisional Constitution, and many political parties existed, but in reality political power was controlled by Yuan Shih-kai and the Northern Warlords.

China, right after the revolution that overthrew the imperial dynasty, and barely organized enough to stand on its feet, joined the First World War in 1917 and declared war on Germany. It was thousands of miles away from the European theater but the Allies wanted China, perhaps, to stop Germany from siphoning off its resources and assets in the Qingdao (Tsingtao) colony in Shandong, China, to help finance its war in Europe.

Germany was defeated, and in the Paris peace conference in 1918, China participated as an equal for the first time, but only to be humiliated by the allies when the former German colony of Qingdao in China was returned not to China but to Japan. That resulted in the May Fourth Movement in 1919. It started as a student movement, and then developed into a youth movement and ultimately a movement among the Chinese intelligentsia in a quest for an ideological basis for China's future development.

At around that time, the October Revolution succeeded in Russia. The world's first socialist country emerged. Intellectuals in China at that time opted for Marxism over other political models.

The first National Congress of the Communist Party of China (CPC) was held in July 1921. With the death of Sun Yat-sen and an attempt by Kuomintang (KMT) to purge Chinese Communist Party (CPC) elements, the two parties' collaboration was ruptured in 1927 and civil war broke out.

In the same year, the Communist Party of China launched its Land Revolution and armed uprising.

Japan invaded China in 1937, leading to the setting up of the anti-Japanese united front of the two parties, the Kuomintang and the Communist Party of China. Chinese people, then united, *defeated Japan the invader.*

After the wars, the peace which the Chinese people had craved for so long did not arrive. Between the two parties in China, KMT and CPC, civil war broke out in June 1946. It was a hard and bitter struggle, but with the Chinese People's Liberation Army occupation of Nanjing in April 1949, Kuomintang's administration in mainland China came to an end.

The People's Republic of China was established on October 1st, 1949 and, led by Chairman Mao Zedong, immediately set about its strength and prosperity, and to spread the wealth among the common people.

It took only half a year for the new nation to stabilize the price of commodities and tackle other serious national issues that had plagued China since ancient times. Land reform was carried out continuously in rural areas, so that more than 300 million peasants obtained about 700 million acres of land. There was great optimism to build a better new China despite many obstacles.

The Korean War broke out in 1950, and China joined the war. Relations between China and Western countries collapsed, China was isolated and sanctioned by them and forced to face a painstakingly long period of total self-reliance.

In 1957, China had just finished its First Five-Year Plan when some of its leaders decided to launch the Great Leap Forward in the misguided belief that it was a shortcut to strengthening the country. This was followed by the tragic Great Chinese Famine which almost crippled the country.

The national economy recovered gradually between 1962 and 1965. However, the country was weakened and power was excessively concentrated in a few individuals.

The Cultural Revolution was initiated officially on May 16th, 1966, which created considerable turmoil and was exploited by counter-revolutionary groups. This resulted in the most destructive upheavals to the country, and injustice to countless people. The national economy was seriously disrupted, social, cultural, and legal institutions were trampled, and the gap in modernization with advanced countries was further widened.

However, in the 1960s and 1970s friendships with other countries in Asia, Africa, and Latin America were continuously expanded, winning China more room for international development. Four months before U.S. President Richard Nixon's visit to China in 1972, China regained its seat in the United Nations.

The Gang of Four responsible for the Cultural Revolution was smashed in October 1976. In 1978, Deng Xiaoping delivered a speech saying: "A party, a country, a nation ... if it only abides by the books, then thinking

Establishment of New China (1949)

Korean War (1950-1953)

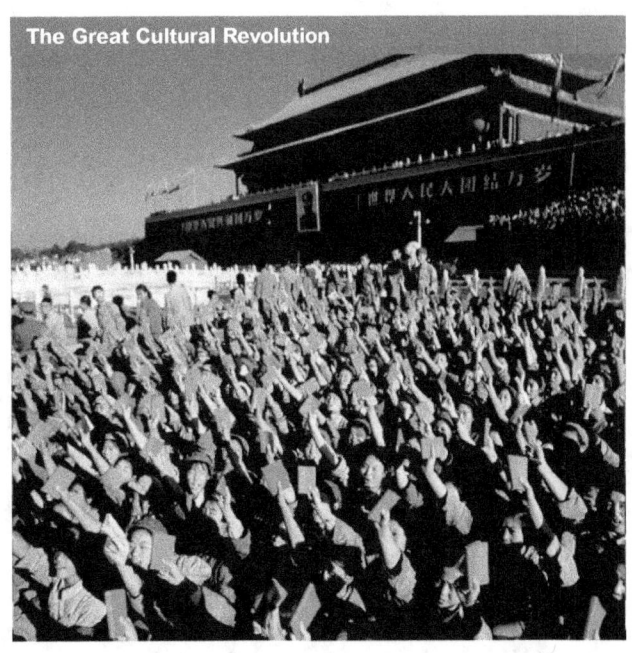
The Great Cultural Revolution

Nixon's Visit to China (1972)

The Four Modernizations (1978)

Agriculture

Industry

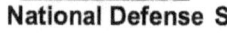
National Defense

Science & Technology

Southern Tour of Deng Xiaoping (1992)

rigidifies, superstition prevails, progress stops, vitality wanes, and the death of the party and nation would be in sight. If reform doesn't proceed now, modernization and socialism would collapse." The speech was described as emancipating the mind, seeking truth from facts, uniting as one and looking forward. The reform and opening up of China officially began.

While meeting with the Prime Minister of Japan, Deng Xiaoping further specified the four modernizations proposed by Premier Zhou Enlai in the 1960s, namely to develop China in the 20th Century as a socialist power with modern agriculture, industry, national defense, and science and technology. He also indicated that the aim was for China to reach about $1,000 per capita by the end of the 20th Century.

Following the creation of four Special Economic Zones, 14 coastal port cities were opened in succession. A more prosperous lifestyle was enjoyed by many ordinary families. Greater creativity and innovation along with respect for knowledge contributed to an upsurge in entrepreneurship and economic success, which benefited even more people through gainful employment.

In 1988, unrest and buying of commodities swept like a tidal wave across China, and the savings of depositors decreased by 30 billion RMB in three months. The critical situation was caused by seismic shifts in the market economy which in turn was triggered by the collapse of old financial systems.

Political turmoil rocked Beijing between May and June of 1989 due to dissatisfaction over certain domestic issues, compounded by international political pressures.

In the face of such internal and external pressures, Deng Xiaoping said the basic route of the reform and opening up will last for a century and cannot be changed. He also dismissed opposition to new things and new ideas and maintained that development was the absolute principle. In 1992, 88-year-old Deng Xiaoping made his famous southern tour and delivered several landmark speeches. "China faces a dead-end if it gives up socialism, refuses reform and opening up, economic development, and improving people's lives gradually," he said. His words continue to exert their influence to this day. The way of reform and opening up was practically institutionalized for China.

From 1989, President Jiang Zemin led China's reform

and opening up efforts. In the ensuing 13 years, the world witnessed dramatic changes in China brought about by the success of its socialist market economy.

China's flag was hoisted in Hong Kong in 1997, indicating that the land ceded forcefully over 150 years earlier had been returned to its rightful owner. Two years later, Macao also rejoined the Motherland.

In 2001 China became a member of the World Trade Organization, affording it a major stepping stone to a higher level of economic growth.

That same year, President Jiang Zemin initiated the "Three Represents" theory—namely, that the Party must always represent the development of China's advanced productive forces (economy), the development of China's advanced culture (culture), and the fundamental interests of the masses (politics).

In 2003, President Hu Jintao declared a manifesto of putting people's interest first, pursuing a sustainable outlook on development, and promoting an all-around development of the individual (social development).

The government committed itself to building a harmonious socialist society, attaching importance to democracy, the rule of law, and harmonious coexistence between human and nature. These social core values were to complement economic, political, and cultural developments.

In 2012, the newly elected Party chief Xi Jinping introduced the "China Dream." He said "Realizing the great renewal of China is the greatest dream for the Chinese people in modern history."

President Xi initiated a campaign to curb extravagance with an all-out effort to tackle corruption. He introduced the dimension of ecological civilization by emphasizing the building of a "Beautiful China," thus completing the five pillars of China's future overall development: political, economic, social, cultural, and ecological considerations.

With these new developments in mind, the China Energy Fund Committee (CEFC) organized a series of forums called "A China Story" at the United Nations to introduce the latest thinking and developments in China to the international community each year in spring after the National People's Congress.

In 2013, *A China Story I* focused on "Sustainable Development and Governance." The seminar told the story of sustainable growth in China which involves a delicate balancing act that takes into account multiple competing forces and needs.

In 2014, the Chinese State Council further announced the New Pathways to Urbanization as an overarching theme of future devel-

Southern Tour of Deng Xiaoping: Results

Deepening of the Reform (From 1989)

China's Sustainable Development (2001-2013)

Xi Jinping—Overall Approach & Beautiful China (2012)

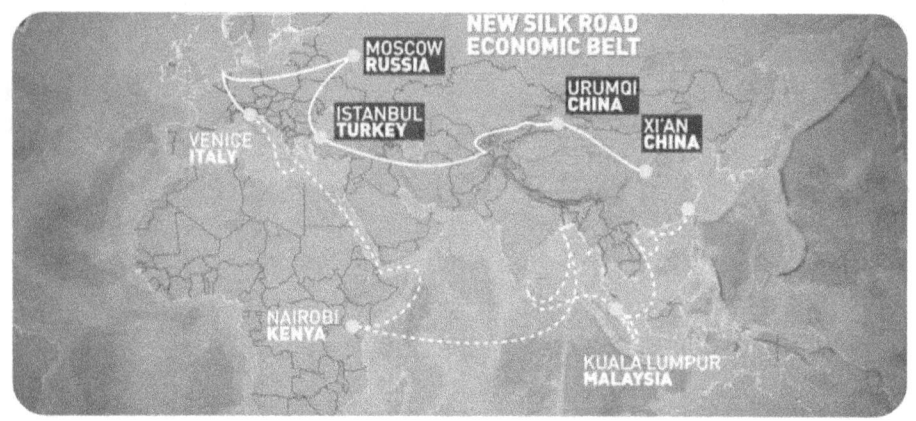

opment embracing all of the five pillars of sustainability, the five pillars being: political, economic, social, cultural, and ecological.

A China Story II in 2014 told the story of how A China Dream could be realized through this New Pathway to Urbanization.

Under President Xi's blueprint for China's future, or the "Four Comprehensives," fulfilling the task of building a moderately prosperous society is a crucial step toward the realization of the "China Dream."

Beginning in 2013, President Xi put forward his strategic vision of building regional connectivity through the Silk Road Economic Belt and the 21st Century Maritime Silk Road.

With the huge opportunities created by the "Belt and Road Initiative" for sustainable development and regional cooperation, the China Energy Fund Committee hosted the last round of *A China Story* entitled "From Diversity, Tolerance to a Community of Common Destiny: The One Belt and One Road Initiative and A New Model of International Cooperation," to tell the story of how countries along the "Belt and Road" can forge stronger diplomatic, strategic and economic ties in building a "community of common destiny." The initiative has organically linked the "China Dream" to the "World Dream," promoting peace and development with far-reaching strategic significance and global impact.

This year, *A China Story IV* is themed on the country's much anticipated 13th Five-Year Plan (FYP) for National Economic and Social Development—the road-map for the nation's economic and social development from 2016 to 2020. This will be a crucial period of transition for China as it steers from a manufacturing, investment and supply-led economy toward a consumer, service, and demand-driven growth.

Guiding the implementation of the current FYP is a philosophy that calls for (1) innovation-driven, (2) balanced, (3) green, (4) open, and (5) inclusive development—the five development concepts.

In terms of targets, over the next five years China aims to (1) maintain a medium to high rate of economic growth; (2) improve living standards and quality of life; (3) raise its level of civilization and improve the social quality of its citizens; (4) significantly improve the quality of its eco-environment; and (5) improve mechanisms

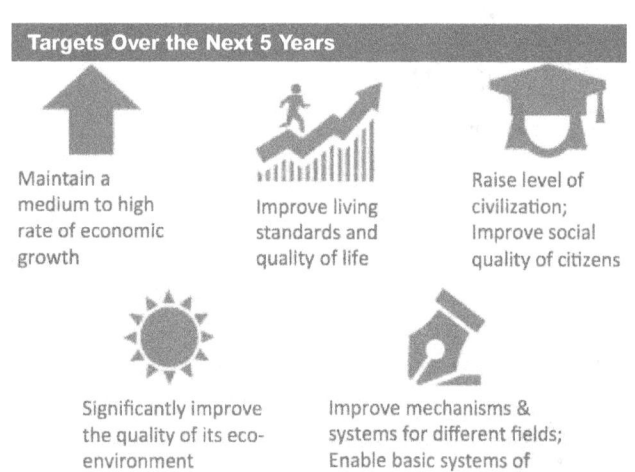

Targets Over the Next 5 Years

Maintain a medium to high rate of economic growth

Improve living standards and quality of life

Raise level of civilization; Improve social quality of citizens

Significantly improve the quality of its eco-environment

Improve mechanisms & systems for different fields; Enable basic systems of city governance to take shape

and systems for different fields and enable the basic systems of city governance to take shape.

More importantly, during this period, the country will seek to achieve, in President Xi's words, the goals of "(1) completing the building of a moderately prosperous society in all respects by 2021 and (2) building China into a modern socialist country that is prosperous, strong, democratic, culturally advanced, and harmonious by the centenary of the People's Republic of China in 2049, so as to realize the Chinese Dream of the rejuvenation of the Chinese nation."

Chinese people love peace and pursue harmony. Such inclinations not only serve its interests, but also that of others they come into contact with. This is the desire of the people, and bespeaks the path of development that China pursues and follows.

So, Ladies and Gentleman, that's China's Story [applause] or 5,000 years of Chinese history in 20 minutes.

Now, going to the substance, let's go on. I can go on and on; if you want to take a break, you can stand up and stretch and do whatever you want, and I'll do likewise.

II. Prologue

The year 2014 is of landmark significance for both China and the world. The world celebrated the 70th anniversary of the founding of the United Nations and began work for a post-2015 development agenda that serves the interests of all countries.

Peace and Development

China will continue with the building of the Silk Road Economic Belt and the 21st Century Maritime Silk Road, known shortly as the Belt and Road Initiative. Originally it was called One Belt, One Road. But then very soon, we understand that there are more than just One Belt, One Road—there are now six of them! And that might be 60 in the very near future. So, we just call it "Belt and Road Initiative" to just give room to future development. As China will continue to build this Belt and Road Initiative, peace and development are the themes of our times.

And also in 2014, President of the United Nations General Assembly, in conjunction with the Secretary-General and the United Nations Alliance of Civiliza-

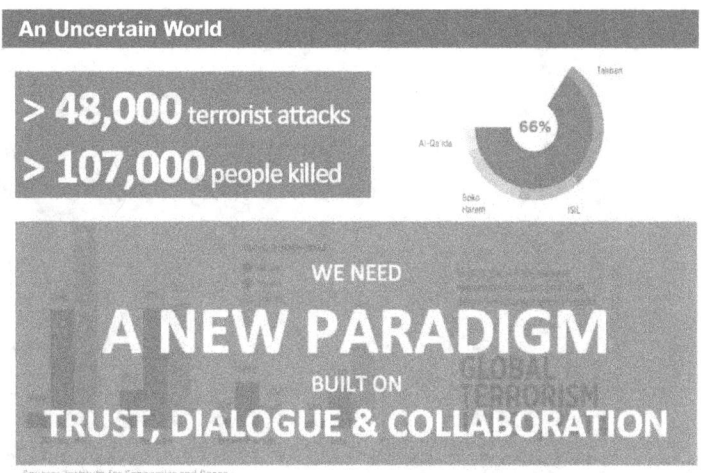

tions, convened a High-Level General Assembly Thematic Debate on "Promoting Tolerance and Reconciliation: Fostering Peaceful, Inclusive Societies and Countering Violent Extremism."

The world is experiencing profound and complex challenges, including the rise of radicalization and violent extremism, against a backdrop of identity-based conflicts, and cultural and religious tensions. Countering these challenges and the threats they pose to populations around the world call for the use of a wide range of approaches to promote tolerance and reconciliation, respect for cultural diversity and freedom of belief, thought and expression. That is to say, we need a new paradigm of development to overcome the zero-sum mentality, to generate collective, inclusive approaches that build on trust, dialogue, and collaboration among countries.

In this context, China's "Belt and Road" initiative does not just symbolize a global vision promoting tolerance and reconciliation among civilizations in Asia, Europe, and Africa. It also represents the global effort of promoting peace and development through international cooperation in the post-2015 development agenda. And that is why the China Energy Fund Committee decided to host these rounds of *A China Story* and also to go around the world, especially to the United States, preaching the content and the virtue of the Belt and Road Initiatives.

'One Belt and One Road'—A New Model of Connectivity

The Belt and Road Initiative is a new model of connectivity, and in 2013, Chinese President Xi Jinping put

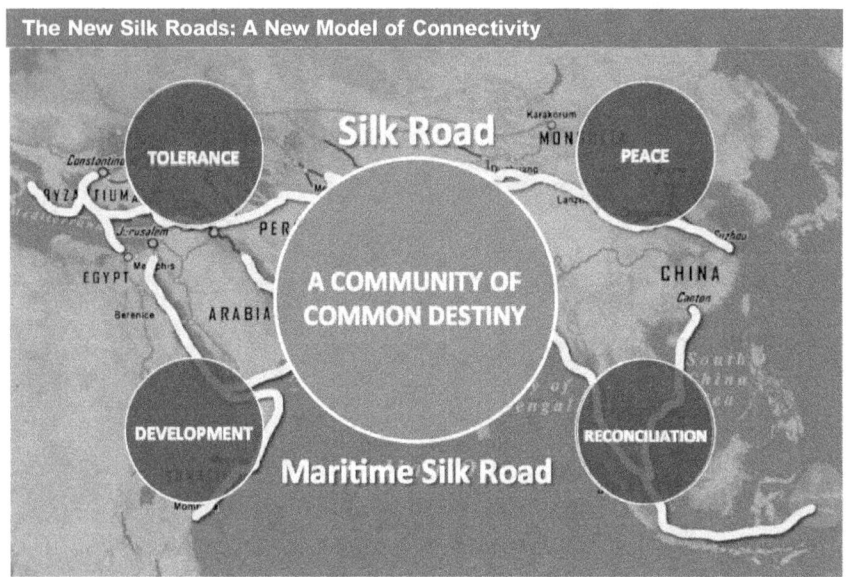

The New Silk Roads: A New Model of Connectivity

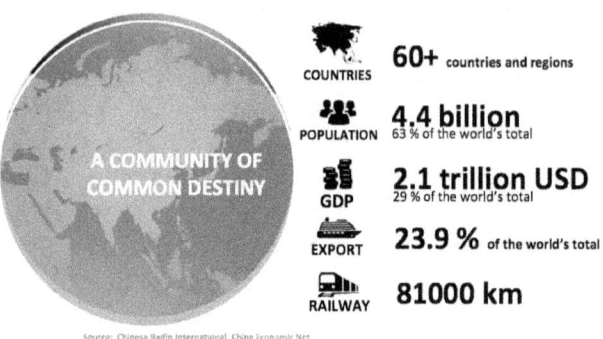

A COMMUNITY OF COMMON DESTINY

COUNTRIES	60+	countries and regions
POPULATION	4.4 billion	63 % of the world's total
GDP	2.1 trillion USD	29 % of the world's total
EXPORT	23.9 %	of the world's total
RAILWAY	81000 km	

Source: Chinese Radio International, China Economic Net

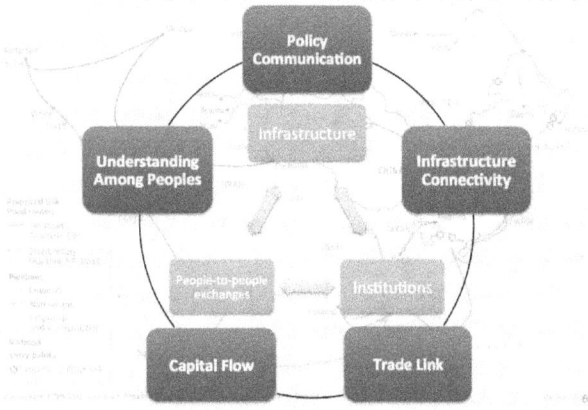

forward his strategic conception of building the "One Belt and One Road" initiatives. This involves constructing an economic and cultural corridor along the ancient Silk Road that extends from the Pacific coast in the East to the Baltic Sea in the West. It is a grand vision

of peace, development, cooperation, and a win-win outcome.

This vision aims to create the most promising economic corridor in the world, directly benefiting a population of 4.4 billion people or 63% of the global population, with a collective GDP of $2.1 trillion that accounts for 29% of the world's wealth. Indeed, it is a grand vision for international cooperation!

Since the initiative was first proposed in 2013, it has been enthusiastically received both at home and abroad. More than 60 states have responded positively for the initiative. Nearly all the major states around the world had agreed or applied to join the Asian Infrastructure Investment Bank (AIIB), to finance and facilitate infrastructure constructions for Asian countries. And the $40 billion Silk Road Fund will soon start investment.

This initiative aims to promote connectivity of the continents and adjacent areas. It is expected in the coming years, that new roads and new railways will be built, new sea lanes and new flight paths will be opened, and oil pipelines and electric grids will be connected. It is a new model of connectivity among peoples! However, connectivity is "not merely about building roads and bridges or making a linear connection of different places on surface. More importantly, it should be a three-dimensional combination of infrastructure, institutions, and people-to-people exchanges and a five-way multi-faceted progress in policy communication, infrastructure connectivity, trade links, capital flows, and understanding among peoples," and may be even more! And should be so!

People-to-People: The Heart of the New Silk Roads

Perhaps "people" is the most crucial, central element. Why is this new initiative for regional cooperation named the "Belt" and "Road" instead of the "Group" and "Plan"? Like the G7 and the Marshall Plan?

The answer is "people." The new initiative is not just a government-to-government or G2G platform, but people-to-people (P2P) exchanges. True, the process is underpinned by government bodies. But the materialization of this grand vision revolves around people. And it was the many ordinary people across the continent that actually connected the East and the West by interactions, exchanges and trade.

Good Will: The Spirit of the New Silk Roads

The second characteristic of this new model of connectivity is "good will."

This initiative is open to all countries and peoples interested in being connected for mutual development, regardless of their forms of government, cultural and religious backgrounds, or geographic location. It is meant to be inclusive, no one is left out.

"Common development" was once the super-glue which bonded different countries along the ancient Silk Roads together, and "equal footing" is what made this "win-win" situation possible. Christians, Muslims, Buddhists, black, white, and yellow peoples were benefited equally from trades and exchanges along the Silk Roads.

So the new initiative should not be construed as China's ambition to become a regional hegemon, but China's "reaching out" offering friendship and peace. More accurately, it is also about China's "bringing in." Motivated by good will, China is inviting peoples and countries along the Silk Roads to build a community of shared interest and common destiny.

We all have different pasts, but we also have a common future to face.

Unlimited Potential: The Vision of the New Silk Roads

Yes, the overall vision of the "One Belt and One Road" initiative is expected to bring about shared economic, cultural and social prosperity. But unlike other regional cooperation projects which have a fixed policy agenda and set mechanism, the "One Belt and One Road" initiative is but a grand vision, providing ample and infinite room for creative solutions and possibilities. It is more ambitious and farsighted, and at the same time more flexible, accommodating, and adaptable to new conditions and challenges, than the ancient Silk Roads. It provides an overarching theme and umbrella under which all sorts of possibilities of cooperation can be made possible.

Ladies and gentlemen,

Today, as we embark on this third year after the Belt

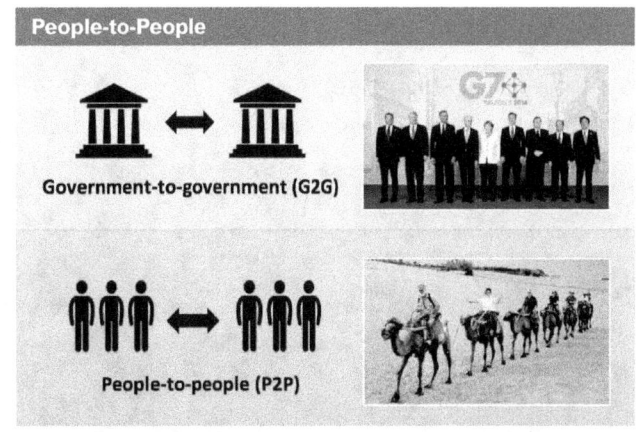

People-to-People

Government-to-government (G2G)

People-to-people (P2P)

Good Will: The Spirit of the New Silk Roads

COMMON   WIN-WIN   EQUAL

OPEN to all countries and peoples
INCLUSIVE
NO ONE is left out
NO ONE takes second place

and Road Initiative, we have to ask: How to identify matching points of economic interest and cooperation opportunities along the "Belt and Road"? What measures should be taken to promote regional trade and economic cooperation? What bottlenecks and weaknesses constrain interconnection? What are the challenges to infrastructure development? Where does the money come from? What sort of roadmaps and institutions should be established to secure common investment, construction, operation and sharing? What areas are important to foster cultural exchanges and mutual understanding between peoples? Is there any new developmental model which can cope with challenges posed by climate change and other environmental problems? And many, many, many more questions will be asked.

We will not be able to answer all these questions today, or even tomorrow, but I hope that our discussions can pave the groundwork of understanding the many implications, significances, and possibilities of this grand vision called the Belt and Road Initiative.

III. Opening Remarks

Now Ladies and Gentlemen,

Let's go to the meat of this Belt and Road, and why China is doing this.

We live in an increasingly thriving world. Standards of living have been improving almost everywhere. Hundreds of millions have been lifted out of poverty, becoming members of societies that are increasingly diverse and inclusive. Human ingenuity, technological advancement, and open markets have given us a world of increasing abundance.

We have made remarkable gains over the course of the last century, and economic measurements evidence this progress. Our increasing prosperity shows us that there are, in fact, enough resources to go around for all of us, including our children.

Looking around the world today, however, we must also acknowledge serious challenges.

Despite the impressive economic growth of recent decades, 1.2 billion people still live in extreme poverty, in conditions that are a far cry from those of the most developed countries. As many as 2.8 billion people lack access to modern energy services. Eight hundred million people remain chronically undernourished. Hundreds of millions still have no access to regular supplies of clean water, while billions live without basic sanitation facilities.

On the other side of the globe, one-third of the food produced globally for human consumption—1.3 billion tons per year—*is wasted*. Developed countries produce dozens and even hundreds of times the emissions and consumption footprints per capita of developing countries. The United States, for example, consumes up to 25% of the world's energy, even though it comprises less than 5% of the world's population.

In 2013, the top 85 multi-billionaires in the world had amassed wealth equivalent to that of the poorest half of the world's population—3.5 billion people.

The top 10% of earners in most advanced economies have fared exceedingly well, while the bottom 10% have continued to fall further, further, and further behind.

These trends repeat themselves not just globally, but also within nations and within cities. Even where there is healthy GDP growth, wealth accumulates primarily at the top. In the United States, despite a doubling of GDP over 30 years, income for low-skilled workers has been stagnant.

The pie has gotten bigger, but apportioned increasingly unfairly: across the globe, across generations, and within nations. This unfair distribution of abundant resources has real and significant consequences. Those who have been left behind, finding no recourse to address systematic unfairness within society, resort to extreme measures to make their voices heard. Ultimately, everyone is harmed by inequality.

What is the origin of these challenges, and how can they be addressed?

These interconnected challenges can be traced back to a broken system of economic development. Since the last millennium, the world's international order has largely been dictated by the disposition of natural resources. Many of the challenges we face today still stem from a zero-sum game of capturing resources for the security and interest of individual countries.

Countries appraising their national security will naturally seek to secure strategic commodities for their internal development, and this concern is only heightened when growth exceeds the local supply of available resources. When confronted with this situation, countries have traditionally expanded their territories overseas, looking for new markets and increased access to resources.

For most of human history, this involved violence, slaves, colonies, and war—with some countries soliciting alliances and annexing territories in the name of religion, civilization, and progress, and others blatantly plundering in search of spoil. Empires and imperialism reigned.

Things changed after the two World Wars. When imperialism and colonialism gave way to democracy and human rights, the answer emerged as "globalization." This new strategy for economic development came to center stage as the default for nations seeking a place at the table of influence.

Globalization deploys capital and investments, trade and goods, people and services, and information across national barriers, as well as reorganizing these entities, to maximize profits. It has proven to be a very effective scheme for amassing great fortune, and it has accelerated growth in the global economy.

Free trade has, however, also come with its share of disadvantages. Most notably, it has disproportionately benefited the capitalist class, while leaving lower-skilled workers struggling to make ends meet. This inequality has not only become a source of social strife and resentment, but also a real obstacle to continued economic growth.

In the developed world, workers now rail against free trade, vilifying offshore workers and foreign investors rather than failing or absent redistribution policies at home.

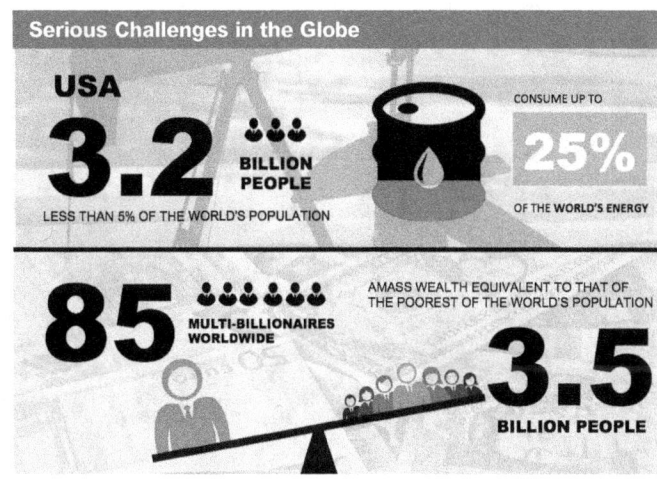

Serious Challenges in the Globe

USA **3.2** BILLION PEOPLE
LESS THAN 5% OF THE WORLD'S POPULATION

CONSUME UP TO **25%** OF THE WORLD'S ENERGY

85 MULTI-BILLIONAIRES WORLDWIDE

AMASS WEALTH EQUIVALENT TO THAT OF THE POOREST OF THE WORLD'S POPULATION **3.5** BILLION PEOPLE

Globalization—Effective Scheme for Amassing Great Fortune and Accelerating Economic Growth

Goods — Service
People — Globalization — Capital
Information

Globalization Is No Longer Able To Advance Human Progress

Our world is now desperately searching for a new model of growth that can replace globalization

– one that is inclusive, far-sighted, holistic, and ready to address global and local inequality, and which will bring people together, creating a common identity through a shared narrative of progress.

CAPITALISM ISN T WORKING

ANOTHER WORLD IS POSSIBLE

One Belt, One Road Initiative

One Belt, One Road Initiative: An answer to the Global need

China Has Chosen a Third Pathway, A Road of Peaeful Co-Development

4 Characteristics
1. GOODWILL
2. SHARING
3. INCLUSIVENESS
4. PEOPLE-to-PEOPLE

THIRD PATHWAY

In the developing world, a failure to share the fruits of progress has resulted in even greater hopelessness and despair. The absence of a future to look forward to, coupled with economic and political uncertainty, has given birth to violent extremism. Today's youth, in particular, are resorting to desperate measures and joining extremist groups.

In either case, the end result is conflict, discord, and instability, within and among nations—all of which tragically have undercut and undermined the drivers of human progress.

Today, globalization is a system in crisis.

The combination of economic downturn, disintegrating social cohesion due to inequality, and environmental woes, have all together led to increasing recognition, around the world, that globalization is a broken system—no longer able to effectively and sustainably advance human progress. An exclusive focus on profits and economic efficiency has failed to translate into the actual well-being of individuals and society. Too many have been left behind.

Our world is now desperately searching for a new model of growth that can replace globalization—one that is inclusive, far-sighted, holistic, and ready to address the challenges of the 21st century. We yearn for a new system that will, in one go, address global and local inequality, and which will bring people together, creating a common identity through a shared narrative of progress.

China's One Belt, One Road Initiative is an answer to this need.

If we aspire to live on this planet happily and peacefully, we must shift towards a more sustainable and inclusive model of development. And those of us on Earth today must share and utilize resources responsibly and sparingly, so that we can grow and develop together. This is the only way that we can achieve long-lasting, peaceful development.

In today's world, it is not possible for one country alone, or one section of society alone, to have and hold all wealth and enjoy the fruits of prosperity. This only leads to resentment from neighbors, who rightfully seek their own path to fulfillment. Inequality leads only to insecurity and instability, ultimately harming both those who have too much, and those who have too little.

What we need today, instead, is a strategy for development anchored in a principle of inclusiveness and sharing. By sharing growth, and securing one another's growth, we can ensure development that is long-lasting and sustainable.

This is the underlying spirit and intention of the One Belt, One Road Initiative: exclusivity and sharing.

Ever since the "reform and opening up" initiated in 1978, China has pursued rapid development by embracing the open market economy. The country's accession to the World Trade Organization in 2001 ushered in a spell of sky-rocketing development. By 2015, China's GDP had multiplied 7-fold since 2000, and 184-fold since 1978. It is now the second largest economic aggregate in the world, after the United States.

But economic prosperity in China, too, came with a heavy toll on the environment and on income equality. With rising wages and escalating land premiums, came renewed public concern for social justice, inequality, and the environment, China has now reached a bottleneck in economic development, just like other maturing economies.

Facing these costs and challenges, China has realized that the current approach to economic growth, with its exclusive focus on profits and returns, is unsustainable. The country understands that only a new mode of growth and development will be able to address fundamental issues such as inequality, lack of natural resources, and excess manufacturing capacities all in one go.

History is full of stories of nations that have opted for colonization or war as answers to faltering growth. China will do neither. It has chosen a third pathway, a road of peaceful co-development driven by a strategy of sharing with its neighbors, and founded on the characteristics of goodwill, sharing, inclusiveness, and people-to-people exchange.

Unlike traditional models of economic development, the Belt and Road Initiative is neither about seeking spheres of influence nor striving for hegemony. It is, instead, about connecting countries and peoples, accommodating differences, embracing diversity, realizing potential, and enabling various goals and prospects.

This is a radical change from business-as-usual under the model of globalization. Under the Belt and Road Initiative, if China has excess capacity and a surplus of funds, it will not leverage them to gain further economic advantages against neighbors. Instead, the country's surpluses will be shared. By helping neighbors grow, and making them into friends that are just as developed as herself, China recognizes that it too will in turn become more stable, more secure, and more prosperous.

The initiative is open to all countries and people interested in being connected for mutual development—regardless of form of government, cultural and religious background, or geographic location. It is guided by a desire to build communities

Characteristic 1: Good Will

Not seeking spheres of influence nor striving for hegemony...

But connecting countries and peoples, accommodating differences, embracing diversity, realizing potential, and enabling various goals and prospects

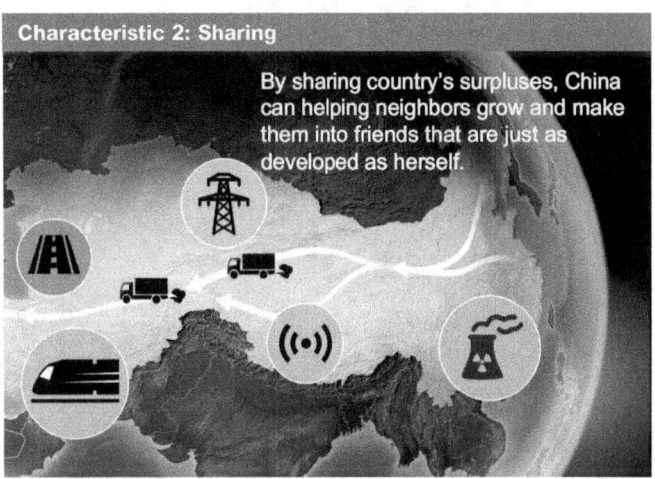

Characteristic 2: Sharing

By sharing country's surpluses, China can helping neighbors grow and make them into friends that are just as developed as herself.

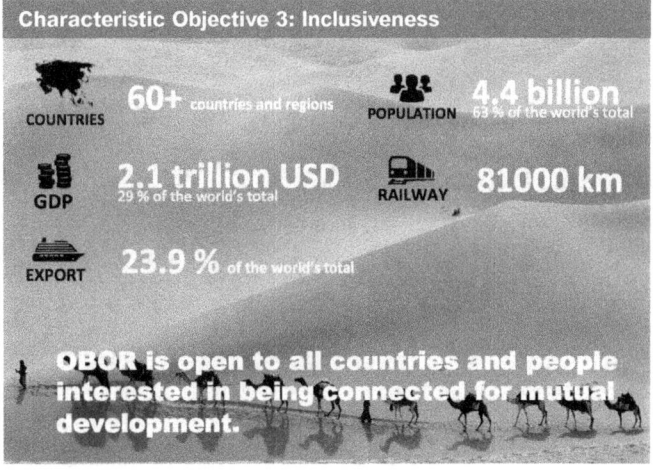

Characteristic Objective 3: Inclusiveness

COUNTRIES 60+ countries and regions
POPULATION 4.4 billion 63 % of the world's total
GDP 2.1 trillion USD 29 % of the world's total
RAILWAY 81000 km
EXPORT 23.9 % of the world's total

OBOR is open to all countries and people interested in being connected for mutual development.

and bring people in, to see others prosper and succeed—just as China has in recent decades. Most of all, it recognizes the potential of everyday people to drive economic growth and serve as a glue for better relations.

This model, which promotes common experience, will ultimately lead to relationships that are meaningful and long-lasting, based on a sense of community rather than competition. In so doing, the Belt and Road Initiative addresses not only economic challenges, but also cultural and social ones—promoting values of sharing and solidarity with all people. The Belt and Road Initiative strengthens the foundations for peace.

How will the Belt and Road Initiative achieve these characteristics?

In its formative stages, the Belt and Road Initiative will rely on major investments in infrastructure-building, putting a call out to the entire world to start steering the global economy back to the basics—real assets, and gradually away from virtual derivatives.

Investing in infrastructure is a proven way to invest in our future, providing a foundation and an impetus for growth and development. It is the bedrock of connectivity, for sustainable development and for poverty eradication.

Fortunately, infrastructure comes in many forms—for the conveyance of goods and people, water, fuel, electricity, and information. All of these are opportunities that the Belt and Road will pursue.

Experts predict that globally, infrastructure demand to 2030 amounts to more than $90 trillion—almost double the $50 trillion worth of today's stock. This means the world needs an investment of $7.7 trillion annually over the next 15 years, to pay not only for infrastructure but also to make it sustainable—which adds a $14 trillion premium. That's a lot of money!

Initial projects will, therefore, likely be state-led, with state enterprises in the forefront, laying down a foundation and launch pad for future growth and development. Privately run medium and small enterprises will, in tandem, start formulating alliances and collaborations with other nations, opening up markets and galvanizing innovation.

The process is kick-started by government organizations

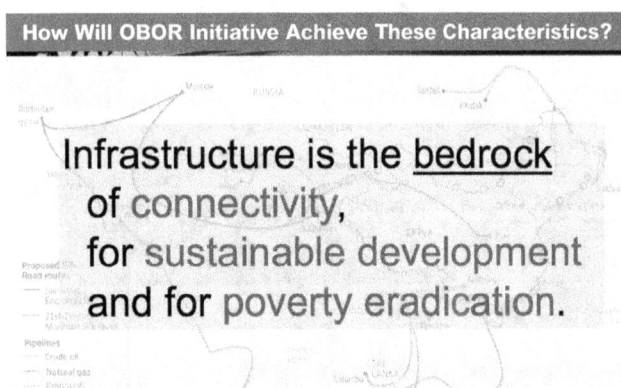

How Will OBOR Initiative Achieve These Characteristics?

Infrastructure is the <u>bedrock</u> of connectivity, for sustainable development and for poverty eradication.

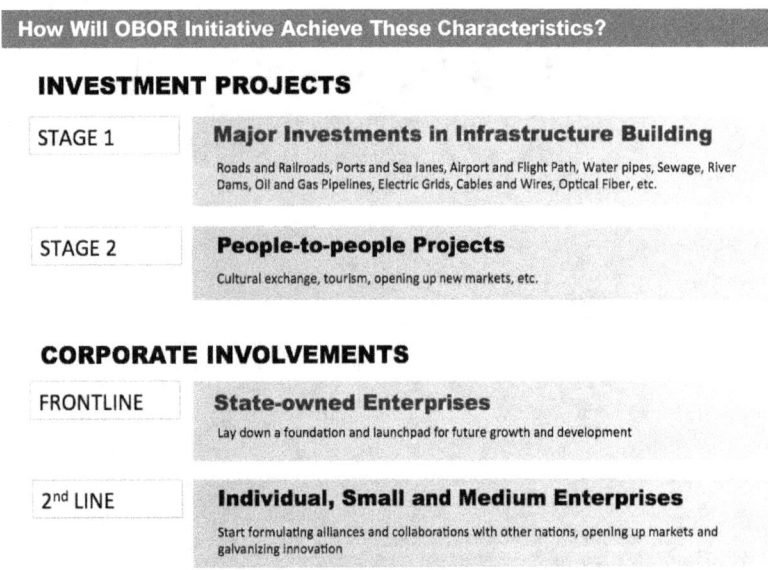

How Will OBOR Initiative Achieve These Characteristics?

INVESTMENT PROJECTS

| STAGE 1 | **Major Investments in Infrastructure Building** |
| | Roads and Railroads, Ports and Sea lanes, Airport and Flight Path, Water pipes, Sewage, River Dams, Oil and Gas Pipelines, Electric Grids, Cables and Wires, Optical Fiber, etc. |

| STAGE 2 | **People-to-people Projects** |
| | Cultural exchange, tourism, opening up new markets, etc. |

CORPORATE INVOLVEMENTS

| FRONTLINE | **State-owned Enterprises** |
| | Lay down a foundation and launchpad for future growth and development |

| 2ⁿᵈ LINE | **Individual, Small and Medium Enterprises** |
| | Start formulating alliances and collaborations with other nations, opening up markets and galvanizing innovation |

only at the beginning. The true materialization of the Belt and Road Initiative's grand vision, however, revolves around people.

So, the infrastructure is really the backbone, forming the skeleton of the Belt and Road Initiative. But the meat, the flesh and the blood comes from the people-to-people interaction; it comes through individual, small and medium businesses.

The first Silk Roads were founded on the interactions of ordinary people across Eurasia, who connected the East and West through dialogue, exchange, and trade. The Belt and Road Initiative, too, will rely on people-to-people networks with neighboring countries, which will be mobilized to forge steadfast bonding and enhance trade.

Business, academic, and social institutions, including cultural and youth organizations, will be key elements of the Belt and Road Initiative. Tourism, too, will be promoted to enhance the sharing of heritage, traditions, and lifestyles, so as to fortify a common experience among peoples.

Individual, small, and medium enterprises, called the ISMEs, will also play a prominent role under the Belt and Road Initiative. Recognizing the new trends of the modern economy, the Belt and Road Initiative will develop an economic environment in which entrepreneurs can thrive—where people can create jobs for themselves as well as others. The Belt and Road Initiative will accomplish this by establishing the foundations for ISMEs—including infrastructure and connectivity backbones, but also socioeconomic policies, and the nurturing of people-to-people networks (such as through conferences and forums).

The success of ISMEs will itself help to advance the Belt and Road Initiative vision. Globalization has largely favored giant international enterprises—which concentrate profits at the top, often at the cost of workers and society. ISMEs, on the other hand, largely tend to be people-based and more intertwined with their workers and communities. They promise to even out income disparities and promote a new distribution of resources—in line with the aims of the Belt and Road Initiative.

A Grand Vision

Finally, unlike other regional cooperation projects which have a fixed policy agenda and a set mechanism, the Belt and Road Initiative is rather a grand vision, providing infinite room for creative solutions and possibilities in implementation.

The Belt and Road Initiative is ambitious and farsighted,

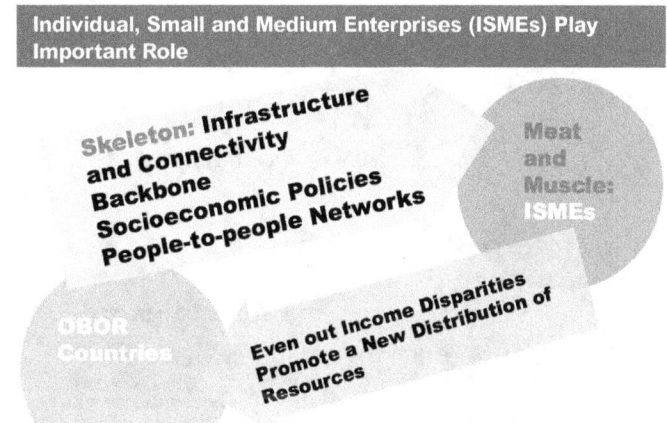

Individual, Small and Medium Enterprises (ISMEs) Play Important Role

Skeleton: Infrastructure and Connectivity Backbone Socioeconomic Policies People-to-people Networks

Meat and Muscle: ISMEs

OBOR Countries

Even out Income Disparities Promote a New Distribution of Resources

OBOR—Creation of World Peace, Friendship and Prosperity

1 Building Roads and Bridges

Connecting Peoples and Communities 2

3 Linking Faiths and Cultures

Joining Lifestyles and Vocations 4

5 Communicating Aspirations and Imaginations

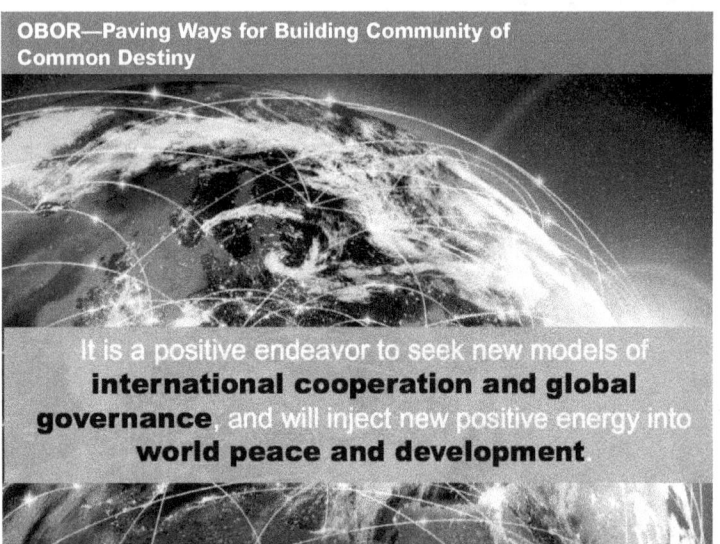

OBOR—Paving Ways for Building Community of Common Destiny

It is a positive endeavor to seek new models of **international cooperation and global governance**, and will inject new positive energy into **world peace and development**

but at the same time also flexible, accommodating and adaptable to new conditions and challenges. It provides an overarching theme and umbrella under which any form of cooperation can be made possible. Governments, businesses, think-tanks, and people can contribute continuously to the initiative, adding to its interpretation, enriching its content, and exploring alternative facets to further cooperation and share benefits.

We all have different pasts, but we also have a common future to face.

The Belt and Road Initiative is a visionary strategy for sustainable growth and development that is inclusive of all mankind. It is not just for China, but a model for all countries and all peoples. Motivated by good will, China is inviting peoples and countries along the Belt and Road Initiative to build a community of shared interest and common destiny—a community where no one is left behind, and where no one has to take second place.

The modern Silk Road teaches us to learn mutual respect and to recognize that despite our different backgrounds and upbringings, there are fundamental values we all hold dear, basic principles we all respect, and core understandings we all embrace. By "reaching out" and "bringing in," we can create a world of peace, friendship, and prosperity.

Ultimately, the Belt and Road Initiative is about building roads and bridges, connecting peoples and communities, linking faiths and cultures, joining lifestyles and vocations, and communicating aspirations and imaginations, in one glorious celebration of diversity of values and accommodation with harmony.

Ladies and Gentlemen, the Belt and Road Initiative is a global challenge, calling for global participation. Through this initiative, China is sending out a most sincere message, loud and clear, of collaboration and partnership, to all our friends and foes from near and afar, to work together to find solutions for sustainable growth for all of humanity. In sharing, we become better partners in advancing our respective goals and achieving our common dreams.

We invite you to be part of this vision and commitment. We want you to be our partner.

IV. Closing Remarks

Centuries ago, John Donne, the English poet, wrote that "No man is an island ... Every man is a piece of the continent, a part of the main." This is more true today, than it ever has been, for all of human history. Our vision for sustainable development should match this reality.

If we aspire to live on this planet happily and peacefully, we must shift towards a more sustainable and inclusive model of development. All must live and pursue growth in ways that are consistent with the

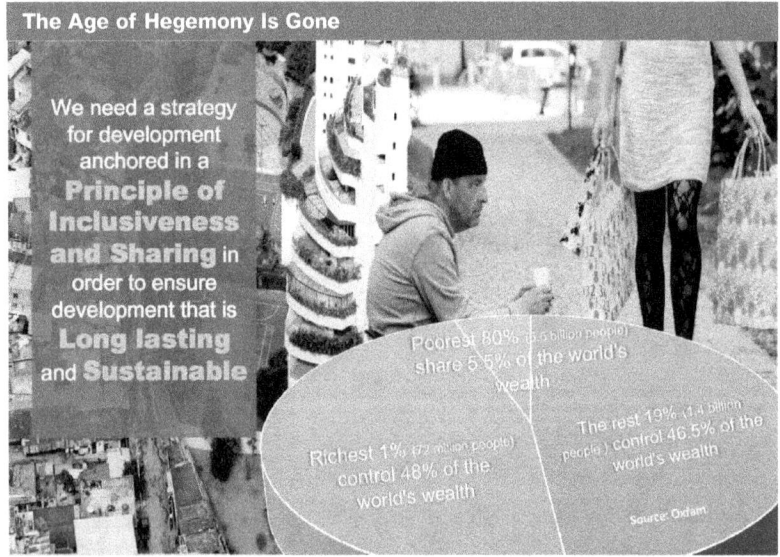

The Age of Hegemony Is Gone

We need a strategy for development anchored in a **Principle of Inclusiveness and Sharing** in order to ensure development that is **Long lasting and Sustainable**

Poorest 80% (5.5 billion people) share 5.5% of the world's wealth

Richest 1% (72 million people) control 48% of the world's wealth

The rest 19% (1.4 billion people) control 46.5% of the world's wealth

Source: Oxfam

needs of future generations. And those of us on Earth today must share and utilize resources responsibly and sparingly, so that we can grow and develop together. This is the only way that we can achieve long-lasting, peaceful development.

The Age of Hegemony Is Gone

In today's world, it is not possible for one country alone, or one section of society alone, to have and hold all wealth and enjoy the fruits of prosperity. This only leads to resentment from neighbors, who rightfully seek their own path to fulfillment. Inequality leads only to insecurity and instability, ultimately harming both those who have too much, and those who have too little.

What we need today, instead, is a strategy for development anchored in a principle of inclusiveness and sharing. By sharing growth, and securing one another's growth, we can ensure development that is long lasting and sustainable.

This is the underlying spirit and intention of the Belt and Road Initiative.

At the opening of the Boao Forum last year, President Xi reaffirmed that China would follow the principle of wide consultation, joint contribution, and shared benefits in promoting the initiative. The programs of development will be open and inclusive, not exclusive. They will be a real chorus comprising all countries along the routes, not a solo performance by China itself. Only through win-win cooperation can we make significant sustainable achievements that are beneficial to all. And China welcomes all countries, including the United States and Japan, to take part in the new initiative as well as in the Asian Infrastructure Investment Bank.

Simply put, the Belt and Road Initiative is neither about seeking spheres of influence nor striving for hegemony. It is about connecting countries and peoples, accommodating differences, embracing diversities, realizing potentials, sharing capacities, and enabling various goals and prospects.

It is a positive endeavor to seek new models of international cooperation and global governance, and will inject new positive energy into world peace and development. It paves the way for building a community of common destiny for all mankind!

The Three 'Knocks'—The World Trying to Understand China

1st Knock Priests and Sinologists — **1583**

2nd Knock Arms and Troops — **1840**

3rd Knock Market Economy and International Trade — **1972**

The Three 'Knocks': The World Tries to Understand China

However, mutual understanding is the most difficult task in international cooperation. In fact, it might take hundreds of years for the West to understand what constitutes "China" and "Chinese-ness." In the past, starting in the 13th century, the West has "knocked" on the ancient door of China at least three times.

The First Knock

In ancient history, the first-ever attempt by the West to understand and open up China began in the Yuan dynasty with Marco Polo (13th Century) and then in late Ming dynasty (16th Century), during which Jesuit priests Matteo Ricci and Joachim Bouvet came to China—Joachim Bouvet was a good friend of Leibniz. And he was the one who corresponded with Leibniz and told him everything about what China has invented, including *I Ching*. And that just accidentally followed in the same way of thinking as Leibniz expressed in the digital binary theory of calculus.

So, that's Bouvet. And they visited China, as priests, bringing with them religion, philosophy, and Western science. This was the first attempt by the Western civilization to come into contact with China. This dialogue was held in the field of philosophy and science between the two giant civilizations of East and West. The late Kangxi era (17th century), however, marked the beginning of years of uncertainty on the grounds of the dispute over religious protocol between China and the Roman Catholic Church. The door for cultural ex-

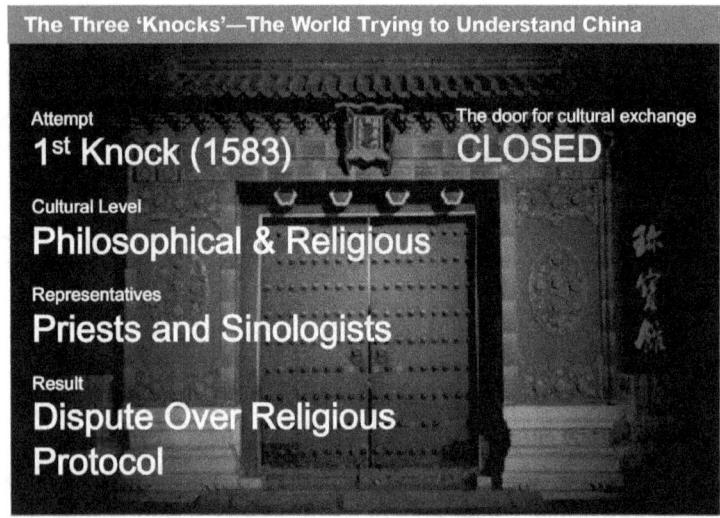

The Three 'Knocks'—The World Trying to Understand China

Attempt
1st Knock (1583)

The door for cultural exchange
CLOSED

Cultural Level
Philosophical & Religious

Representatives
Priests and Sinologists

Result
Dispute Over Religious Protocol

Attempt
2nd Knock (1840)

The door for cultural exchange
OPEN BUT NOT AT WILL

Cultural Level
Technological

Representatives
Arms and Troops

Result
Wars and Revolutions

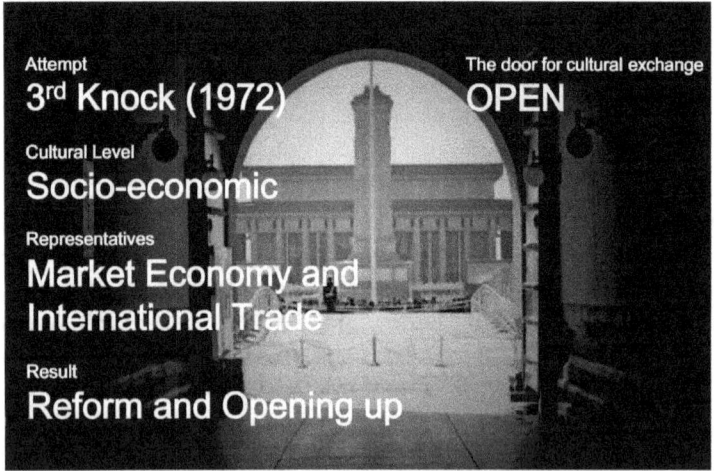

Attempt
3rd Knock (1972)

The door for cultural exchange
OPEN

Cultural Level
Socio-economic

Representatives
Market Economy and International Trade

Result
Reform and Opening up

change was callously closed, leading to a state of mutual disconnection.

The Second Knock

Modernization of human society became an irresistible historical trend, but the Chinese—still complacent at that time in national peace and splendor—were completely unaware of the misfortune about to befall them. Aiming to enrich themselves with natural resources through their military supremacy, Western countries forcibly expanded colonialism to the East. The second "knock" came in 1840, when Britain invaded China and launched the First Opium War. China's doors were pried ajar against her will.

Throughout the recent 2,000 years of Chinese history, GDP of China ranked first globally. Even following the two Opium Wars, in 1840 and 1860, when China lost to the British, China's GDP managed to constitute one-third of the world's total volume. When China lost the First Sino-Japanese War in 1894, China's GDP was five times higher than that of Japan. China then realized that its GDP represented prosperity and not proportionate national strength. China was big and prosperous, but not strong and healthy.

Ever since 1840, for more than 100 years, after being brought to its knees by the guns and warships of the West, China was awakened, suddenly realizing that it had to catch up with the Western world, and has since striven successively to strengthen its military, economy and politics, with a steadfast goal of rejuvenation of the Chinese people.

The Third Knock

The third "knock" on the door of China came in the midst of the Cold War in 1972, when Richard Nixon from the U.S.A. visited China, offering an olive branch to China to integrate into the global economic system of the era.

When Deng Xiaoping came into power, China began walking down the path of development of a socialist market economy with Chinese characteristics. With rapid economic advancement, China moved towards a moderately well-off society.

This was perceived as the third attempt of opening up China by the West. Unlike the previous two attempts, China was introduced to Western social systems and concepts of market economy and international trade. Nixon's visit kicked off a string of multi-faceted social contacts between China and the West. This was of vital importance to China's modernization as it was conducive to integrating such an ancient giant civilization into the modernized international system.

The Third Knock by China: A New Silk Road to the World Dream

Looking back in recent history, the West had knocked on China's door three times. But China has also knocked on the door of the West at least twice: first, during the Han Dynasty (Second Century B.C.) when Emperors governed with non-interference, peaceful development, and dispatched envoys to forge the first contacts with the West, and opened up the Silk Road on land led by Zhang Qian (beginning 139 B.C.), offering trade and peace.

The second knock came from the Ming Dynasty (A.D. 1403-1435) when Admiral Zheng He and his powerful fleets were sent to sail from the South China Sea to the Indian Ocean, to Africa and, arguably, even to America, some 71 years before Christopher Columbus.

The Chinese people are a peace-loving people. Whereas Julius Caesar said what he said, the Chinese people said what they want to say! "We make friends. We don't conquer, we make friends and go home. No colonies. China never had colonies, through 5,000 years of history, China never had colonies, nobody was enslaved.

The 21st Century will see us embarking on the third Silk Road. The grand vision of the "Belt and Road" is the third "Knock" on the door of the West by China. Indeed, it is a Big Bang on our neighbor's door.

When Belt and Road Initiative was launched in 2013, we knocked on the American doors,—which did not open. [laughter] And today, we are banging on Mr. Trump's doors, and chanting "Open Sesame." [laughter, applause]

Outlines for the New U.S. Administration to Consider

1. Consider using OBOR as a platform to spearhead initiatives and programs conducive to a closer cooperation between China and the USA

2. Realign trade agreements (with Pacific countries and Atlantic countries) to accommodate OBOR

3. Adjust US's position in development banks and promote their capacities to assist in financial arrangements to support infrastructure development

4. Provide leadership to assure security on land and at sea for OBOR infrastructures and related projects

5. Leverage US's role in International Organizations to support and promote the spirit and effort of the OBOR Initiative

After today's discussion, I must say that our "open sesame" is a big yell to the new American administration to reconsider the Belt and Road Initiative as an impetus to rethink and realign the U.S. foreign policy for the new century.

I can summarize the salient points and outline the areas for the new administration in America to consider, as follows.

1. Consider using Belt and Road Initiative as a platform to spearhead initiatives and programs conducive to a closer cooperation and fostering of good will between China and the United States. You know, actually, China and the United States have very little against one another. We have no territorial conflicts. We are on the east and on the west, we are separated by oceans and fish [laughter]—and there is no reason why we should be enemies. So, there are always reasons we should work together. And in the past, it's always been a platform about democracy, then "human rights"; then trade, then climate change. And after climate change, then what? Belt and Road Initiative.

2. Realign trade agreements with Pacific countries and Atlantic countries to accommodate the Belt and Road Initiative. Especially nowadays, when the TPP has been shelved, and it's time that we know we should come up with some alternative to the TPP and the TTIP as well, considering trade.

3. Adjust the U.S. position on development banks—especially the IMF and World Bank, and Asia Develop-

China
Dream

For thousands of years, Chinese had a dream.

ment Bank as well—and promote their capacities to assist in financial arrangements to support infrastructure development along the Belt and Road.

4. Provide leadership to ensure security on land and at sea for Belt and Road Initiative infrastructures and related projects; and

5. Leverage U.S. roles in international organizations to support and promote the spirit and effort of the Belt and Road Initiative.

Ladies and Gentlemen: The two previous Silk Roads traded tea, silk, spices, exotic fruits, jewelry and gold. The 21st Century Silk Road trades for, apart from creative ideas, it trades views and perspectives, traditions and legacies; it trades *values*. It exchanges *kindness*. It offers peace.

This modern Silk Road travels not only by sea or by land, or goes from one place to another, but travels through the inner workings of the human hearts and

China Dream

"Realizing the great renewal of China is the greatest dream for the Chinese people in modern history."

Xi Jinping
November 29, 2012

minds, connecting lives and souls, and driven by a desire to capture the advantages of peaceful cooperation and competition.

This modern Silk Road is a visionary strategy for sustainable growth and development that is inclusive of all mankind. It is not just for China or for the U.S.A., but a model for all countries and all peoples. Motivated by goodwill, China is inviting the American people, and U.S.A. the country, to build a community of shared interest and common destiny—a community where no one is left behind, and where no one has to take second place.

This modern Silk Road teaches us to learn mutual respect and to recognize that despite our different backgrounds and upbringings, there are fundamental values we all hold dear, basic principles we all respect, and core understandings we all embrace. By "reaching out" and "bringing in," we can create a world of peace, friendship, and prosperity.

Ultimately, the Belt and Road Initiative is about building dreams and realizing them. The Belt and Road Initiative is an affirmative answer to questions over civilization's future, setting out a path to a world where everyone can live spiritually fulfilling lives: free of want, free of fear, in harmony with nature, and in long-lasting times of peace.

V. Epilogue

Because, Ladies and Gentlemen, for thousands of years, Chinese had a dream.

In 2012, China's new leader, Xi Jinping, laid out his vision of the "the China Dream" with these words: "Realizing the great renewal of China is the greatest dream for the Chinese people in modern history."

And to achieve it, China must adhere to the path of socialism with Chinese characteristics. This path is hard-earned, with impressive progress over the past 30 years of reform and opening-up; through the continuous exploration over 60 years since the establishment of a new China; in the often painful 170 years of the development process of the Chinese nation in modern times; and against a backdrop of the 5,000 years' legacy of an ancient civilization.

Significantly, the path to the China Dream is

anchored in China's deep cultural heritage and ancient historical roots.

The China Dream

In every dynasty, leaders and heroes had had their respective China dreams. Throughout Chinese history, the golden eras in the Han, Tang, Ming and Qing Dynasties all brought progress and prosperity, taking Chinese civilization to new heights as we chased that brilliant but elusive Chinese dragon.

And so it was beginning with the pain of the Opium Wars, moving into the Self-Strengthening Movement of 1860, the Hundred Days' Reform of 1898, the 1911 Revolution of Sun Yat-sen, the May Fourth Movement in 1919, the establishment of the Communist Party of China in 1921, to the founding of New China in 1949, through a series of modernization movements in the '50s and '60s, the "two bombs and one satellite" goal, to the reform and opening up, and the space dream, the World Trade Organization dream, the Olympic dream, the World Expo dream.

Mao Zedong's "Serving the People," Deng Xiaoping's "Xiaokang Society," President Jiang Zemin's "Three Represents," President Hu Jintao's "Scientific Development Concept," President Xi Jinping's "Five Pillars of Development" and the "Four Comprehensives," have been all about the dreams of modernization, after this ancient civilization had been repeatedly challenged by the achievements and mightiness of the West.

Yes, we Chinese never ceased dreaming! And we have realized many of our dreams through the ages! But this is a self-renewal process for Chinese culture over five millennia, with the Chinese people always wishing to better our lot, through hard work and commitment to our traditional values. To heal old wounds, stand up from where we fell, rejuvenate and renew our outlook on our collective destiny, are the innate qualities of our culture and the built-in quality of this civilization.

The China Dream is a national dream, and also a very personal one to every Chinese. However, no personal dream is fulfilled by oneself alone. Every dream must ultimately involve the country and society in some way. Thus, your dream affects mine, and vice versa. But "the

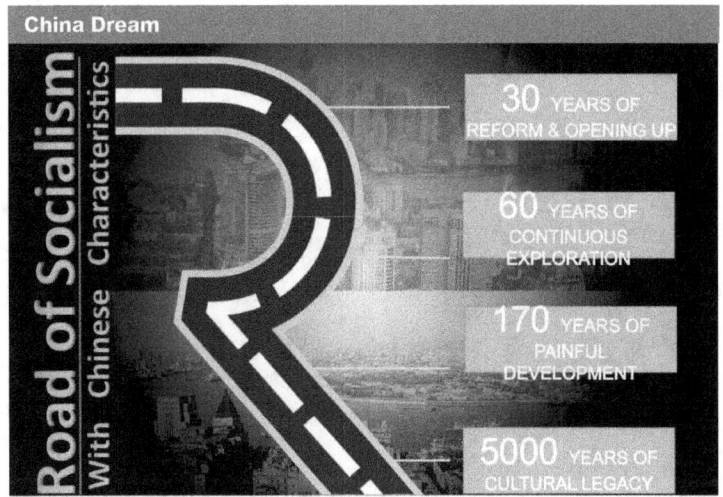

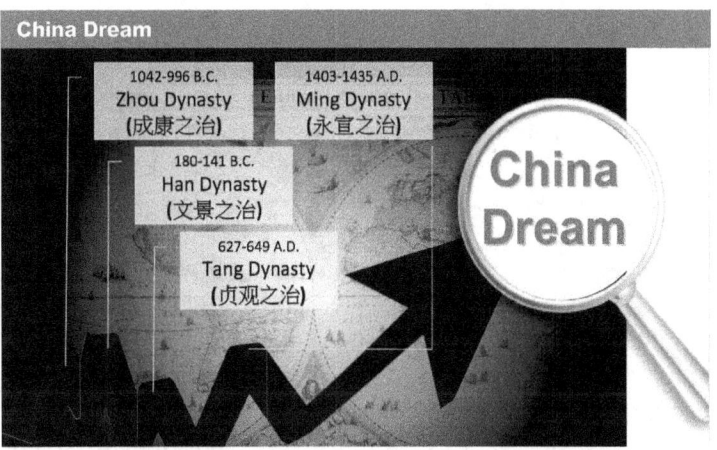

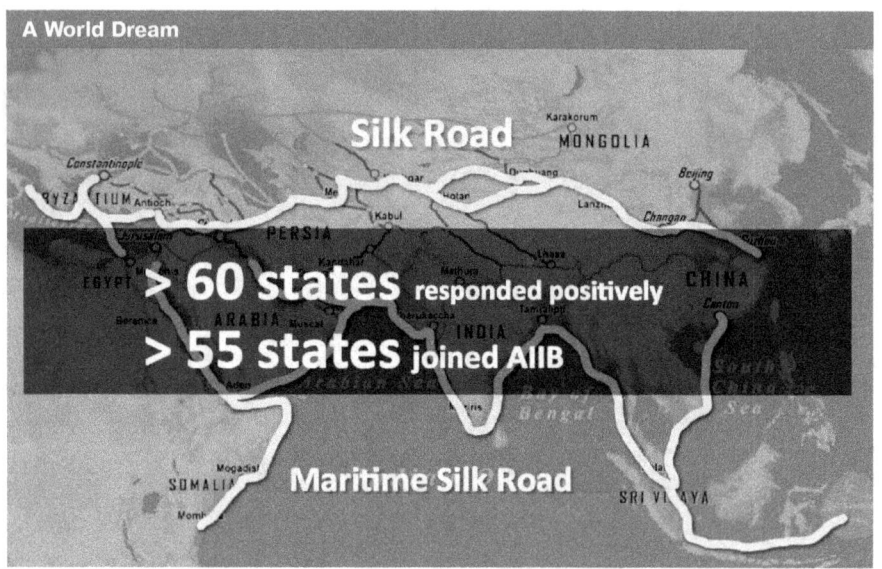

Silk Road

MONGOLIA

> 60 states responded positively

> 55 states joined AIIB

Maritime Silk Road

However, closer ties among neighbors of unequal sizes often spark suspicions of intentions of geopolitics. It is not surprising that some commentators labeled the Belt and Road Initiative a Chinese version of the Marshall Plan, which seeks to establish its spheres of influence in the "Eurasian Heartland."

Such misunderstandings and prejudice are normally rooted in the rigid and old-fashioned patterns of zero-sum thinking. As Chinese Foreign Minister Wang Yi said earlier this year,

China's Belt and Road Initiative is both much older and much younger than the Marshall Plan. Comparing one to the other is like comparing apples to oranges. The initiative is older because it embodies the spirit of the ancient Silk Road, which had a history of more than 2,000 years. The initiative is younger because it is born in the age of globalization. It is the product of inclusive cooperation, not a tool of geopolitics, and must not be viewed with the outdated Cold War mentality.

At the opening of the Boao Forum three weeks ago, President Xi has reaffirmed that China would follow the principle of wide consultation, joint contribution and shared benefits in promoting the initiative. The programs of development will be open and inclusive, not exclusive.

Simply put, the Belt and Road Initiative is neither about seeking for spheres of influence nor striving for hegemony. It is about connecting countries and peoples.

It is a positive endeavor to seek new models of international cooperation and global governance, and will inject new positive energy into world peace and development.

The Belt and Road Initiative is all about building dreams, sharing dreams and realizing them. This dream is not only the dream of 1.3 billion Chinese over 5,000 years, it is also a world dream. It is a dream of peace under heaven, and the world as one.

This dream belongs to all of us. It belongs to you, and it belongs to me.

Thank you. [applause]

China Dream" represents the Chinese people's collective desire, and encompasses the essence of many individuals' visions and expectations.

The grandest dreams, at the level of the nation and state, are peace, security and prosperity. Dreams of much smaller scale, reflecting those of the man in the street, are food, housing, education, a decent standard of living, old age security, and personal respect and dignity. Such dreams of China's 1.3 billion people have interwoven themselves to form a grand dream—the modern dream of China.

That Dream is for China's prosperity and strength, national rejuvenation, economic development, political integrity, cultural vibrancy, happiness for all, a harmonious society, and ecological wellbeing. It is a national calling to a common purpose and for a collective approach in our pursuits.

A World Dream

Indeed, the China Dream is an inseparable part of the World Dream. China is an important member of the international community. China cannot develop itself in isolation from the rest of the world. And vice versa, the rest the world cannot enjoy prosperity and stability without China's participation.

To promote connectivity of the Asian, European and African continents, President Xi put forward the initiative of jointly building the Silk Road Economic Belt and the 21st-Century Maritime Silk Road during his foreign visits in 2013, and won broad support from neighboring countries.

HELGA ZEPP-LAROUCHE

World Land-Bridge: Mankind's Next Great Task

Below is an edited transcript of an address by Helga Zepp-LaRouche to the Dec. 10, 2016 Schiller Institute Conference in New York City. It is preceded by a transcript of the introduction of Zepp-LaRouche by moderator Dennis Speed.

Dennis Speed: One thing struck me about what Dr. Ho just said, at the end of his slide show, "The Inexhaustible Road to Self-improvement and Development." I'd like to say something about the next speaker, the founder of the Schiller Institute, Helga Zepp-La-Rouche. At a very young age, she went to China, on an unauthorized visit at a time that you weren't supposed to be able to go there. She became involved in the economics and politics of Lyndon La-Rouche. She is married to Lyndon LaRouche. But the thing that characterizes her is that she believes in the idea of living with genius and paying the price of living with genius. Now, the price of living with genius is that you have to give up being stupid, and that's a very seductive thing.

What she did, in 1983, when Lyndon LaRouche successfully convinced the Reagan Administration to adopt the Strategic Defense Initiative, which was a new strategic platform which could have ended the age of nuclear madness, Helga proposed to elements of the United States government that they have a corresponding cultural initiative, and that this cultural initiative would seek to look for the best in all nations and advance, together with the Russians and others, the cause of a community of principle.

They rejected that; the United States State Depart-

Helga and Lyndon LaRouche in Berlin in October, 1988. He was in Berlin to issue his forecast of the imminent breakup of the Soviet bloc, and to propose a reconstruction plan for all of Europe.

EIRNS/Dean Andromidas

ment and others rejected that because they didn't have the vision to see what she already saw.

And so, she founded the Schiller Institute during the summer of 1984, to carry out that initiative herself. This was a civilizing influence on the United States. It was a civilizing influence throughout the world as a whole. But she used poet Friedrich Schiller, the Poet of Freedom, and introduced Americans to him, his work, and not only that, very soon after that 1984 founding of the Schiller Institute, she pioneered work with the scientist Krafft Ehricke, one of the most important physicists and visionaries of the 20th Century.

She did many other things. But at the point that the Berlin Wall came down in November 1989, and her husband Lyndon La-Rouche was in jail, the two of them cooked something up, which at that time was known as the European Productive Triangle, which subsequently became known as the Eurasian Land-Bridge. It was a campaign and initiative that she was qualified to do, and advance, as no one else was.

We talked earlier about how in 1996, Helga spoke in Beijing at a conference on the New Silk Road, and then became known as the "Silk Road Lady" all over the world. She was here many times in New York City, in 1997 and '98 in particular advancing that cause.

By living with genius, in the form both of the people she has known personally, and the people she has advocated who are her friends that she never met, like Schiller, and Nicholas of Cusa and others, there's been a new cultural platform implicitly established in the world. Now, we're in a new era, where the power of ideas, that people like Xi Jinping have not only represented, not only embodied, not only advanced, not only improved, but have made available to everyone else on the planet, which shows a kind of love for humanity, which is indispensable in real leadership.

It's always my honor to introduce the founder and head of the Schiller Institute, Helga Zepp-LaRouche. [applause]

Helga Zepp-LaRouche: I will try to be brief because much time has been lost already [with technical problems], and when Dr. Ho said that in order to understand Chinese-ness you have to be Chinese, I was actually considering, you know, maybe given the fact that I was in China the first time in 1971, 45 years ago, maybe we as a whole movement are already Chinese, or maybe it is also the other way around, that what China is proposing now, with the New Silk Road/One Belt, One Road Initiative is actually more human, and it is the problem that the trans-Atlantic world has lost the correct way.

I came back from this trip to China—which also took me to Africa and some other Asian countries—I spent several months in China during the Cultural Revolution, and I came back from this trip, having seen the underdevelopment of China and many other countries—with the idea that the world could not stay like that. And when I came back and found the theories of Lyndon LaRouche, it was very clear that that was the road to go. And then, we spent the next several decades to make very concrete development plans for Africa; we worked with López Portillo on a Latin American integration program. We worked with Indira Gandhi on a 40-year development plan for India. Already in 1975, Mr. LaRouche proposed an International Development Bank. If you compare all of these projects which we promoted in hundreds of conferences internationally over these decades, this is exactly what China is doing now.

So, is it an affinity that we are Chinese, or is it that the Chinese are really part of the Schiller Institute? Or is it the case that it is the natural development of mankind to take that road, and it's only the relics of the oligarchical system of the trans-Atlantic sector, which has prevented this natural development from occurring?

Dennis, since, you mentioned Krafft Ehricke—he actually had this idea of an evolution of mankind which started with the idea that life developed from the oceans through photosynthesis, to land, and then higher species developed with a higher energy-flux density in their metabolisms. Eventually man appeared and man started to settle first near oceans and rivers. And then through the development of higher levels of infrastruc-ture—roads, canals, eventually trains—the landlocked areas of the planet would all be opened up.

The whole idea of the World Land-Bridge—the New Silk Road becoming the World Land-Bridge—is the completion of that phase of natural development. And naturally, the next phase of this development is the infrastructure development of nearby space: First the Moon, then other heavenly bodies, and this will be the natural development of civilization.

So what China is doing, based on its 5,000-year tradition is really what is inherent in the human species. And as I said, it is the trans-Atlantic sector which has left the correct path.

And I just want to pose this as a real challenge, because anybody who has been in China or is now involved in the New Silk Road dynamic—this amounts to now 100 nations and large institutions which have undertaken the most unprecedented development perspective since Xi Jinping put the New Silk Road on the agenda in 2013. Now all the countries which are a part of it, are completely optimistic, looking to the future with a bright perspective. But it is the old geopolitical interests in Europe, and also in the United States, that are definitely resisting this perspective, because it goes against everything they have been trying to impose in the last decades.

Now this trans-Atlantic world order, as we all are acutely aware, is very rapidly collapsing. The Brexit was the first drumbeat of a world revolution opposing the globalization. You had the election of Mr. Trump, which was primarily a rejection of what Obama and Hillary Clinton stand for.

The Italian "no" in the referendum again represents all the people who were left behind by globalization—which has just made the rich more rich and the poor, poorer. And this process will continue until the injustice associated with this present trans-Atlantic system is overcome.

Right now there is an unbelievable situation in the United States, where the official office for health statistics just released a report indicating that from 2014-2015, the life expectancy of Americans has dropped for the first time! This has never happened in the civilized world, anywhere. As the result of a drop from 76.5 to 76.3, for the ages of men, they are now not living as long. The drop is a little bit less for women. All the major diseases in the United States have increasing death rates: 8 out of 10 major diseases now result in more deaths than before, and this is in the formerly most advanced country.

Fusion power research in China: Experimental Advanced Superconducting Tokamak (EAST).

In Europe, it's not much better because in Greece, as a result of the Troika policy on debt repayment, 45% of the people have reached the poverty level, and in Italy, 50% of the youth are unemployed. In Calabria, youth unemployment is 65%, and what the European Central Bank (ECB) is doing right now in response to the "no" vote of the Italians in the referendum, is to open the monetary flood gates in a way which is absolutely unprecedented: quantitative easing, state printing of money, which is exactly what the Reichsbank did in 1923 in Weimar Germany.

So, I don't want to go through more of these symptoms of collapse, because with the new paradigm on the table, I think the only way mankind will get out of this crisis is by convincing the Americans and the Europeans that it is in their best interests to join with China and go back to those policies which were original American policies—the Alexander Hamilton American System of economy, which was repeated by John Quincy Adams, by Lincoln, by Franklin D. Roosevelt, and which my husband, Mr. LaRouche again formulated in 2014 in the package of the famous Four Laws: First Glass-Steagall, then go to a credit system, and then have an international credit system to finance long-term development projects; and fourthly to institute a science-driver for a crash fusion program and joint space cooperation.

These are the tasks in front of us and I think everything will really depend on our ability to quickly promote this policy. The world is not in as much of a danger of World War III as it was the day before the U.S. election, because Trump has promised a lot of things: He has promised to normalize the relationship between the United States, Russia, and China; he has promised to implement Glass-Steagall; he has announced that he wants to have an infrastructure program which will give America the most modern infrastructure—now that is quite a task given the abysmal condition of the infrastructure in the United States.

The United States will have to do a lot of development to catch up with China. which has already built 20,000 kilometers of high speed rail, and will have 50,000 km by the year 2020. But as Mme. Fu Ying said recently in New York, this idea of having an infrastructure program for the United States, can be the bridge with the One Belt, One Road of China.

However, there are many obstacles. For example, in Europe you still have a Green paradigm in many countries, especially Germany, which is not exactly the green vision of China. China wants to have a clean environment, which is absolutely correct to do, but in other countries it is a different conception: It is the idea of what they call "sustainable development" which really is a code word for "no development." And there are many, many obstacles to overcome. However, I think the perspective is there, because of what China has done in terms of the crash program for fusion. China is the only country which is investing more funds into fusion energy. The EAST project in Hefei at the plasma research institute reached 100 seconds of plasma stable condition a couple of months ago, so China is on the right track. China has the most advanced space program. The Chang'e-5 mission next year will bring materials from the Moon back to Earth. One year later, the Chang'e-4 mission in 2018 will go to the far side of the Moon, with the perspective of eventually mining helium-3 from the Moon for a fusion economy on the Earth.

And it is really this kind of future orientation—that the next phase of evolution is the colonization of space and this must be a project of international cooperation—which is really the way how we will get mankind out of this present danger.

I don't want to make a longer speech than that. There are many things to be said, but I would like to open it for the discussion.

OBOR Brings New Life to Central Asia: Kazakhstan in Focus

by Ramtanu Maitra

Dec. 12—The 2013 New Silk Road initiative of China's President Xi Jinping, called One Belt One Road (OBOR), or the Belt and Road Initiative, is anchored in the idea of developing land and sea transport corridors stretching from China's cities to Europe. The overland routes wend their way through Central Asia. The five Central Asian nations—Kazakhstan in the north, bordering Russia, and to its south, Turkmenistan, Uzbekistan, Tajikistan, and Kyrgyzstan—are all destined to benefit from China's OBOR initiative and could become an economic hub within Eurasia.

Three of the five share a border with China, and China has laid railroads through its vast western province, Xinjiang, to these borders with Kazakhstan, Kyrgyzstan, and Tajikistan, where it is setting up dry ports along these borders.

Government of Kazakhstan

Kazakhstan's Nurly Zhol program includes the construction of new cities, new housing in existing cities, utilities, roads, rails, and bridges. Here, President Nursultan Nazarbayev points out features on a road model.

Railroads, Pipelines and Financing

Even years before President Xi's official declaration in 2013, China had already begun to invest heavily in the infrastructure to link up with Central Asia. It has built a railway corridor that originates at the Pacific port of Lianyungang on the Yellow Sea, traverses Kazakhstan, and continues on to Russia, Poland, and Germany. This land-bridge reduces shipment time and cost between China and Europe.

China has also built a rail line that branches off to the south from the China-Kazakhstan railroad near Astana, the capital of Kazakhstan, goes into Uzbekistan and Turkmenistan, and ends at Tehran, Iran. This branch can be called the China-Central Asia-West Asia corridor.

It is evident from these developments that OBOR has put special emphasis on utilizing Kazakhstan as an important hub. For China, Kazakhstan is of immediate importance. The China-Central Asia natural gas dual pipeline of 1,840 kilometers ("Lines A and B") was built in 2008-2010 to bring in 30 billion cubic meters of gas from Turkmenistan, Uzbekistan, and Kazakhstan. A third pipeline of larger diameter, Line C, parallel to the first two, was built in 2012-2014 and delivers an additional 25 billion cubic meters.

In September 2013, President Xi announced the plan to revive the ancient Silk Road and connect China with Central Asia, the Middle East, and Europe, and a year later in November 2014, in a meeting with Asian leaders, Xi committed $40 billion to this ambitious project, designed to "break the connectivity bottleneck" in Asia. The China-led Asian Infrastructure Investment Bank (AIIB), officially launched in June 2015 with a capital of $100 billion, can provide some additional financial muscle for these initiatives.

KAZAKHSTAN

New Rail Corridors

While the two rail corridors described earlier are already operational, China has worked on two more corridors to tie up with Central Asia. One is the proposed high-speed, narrow-gauge railroad to Khorgos (Horgos), the eastern Kazakhstan dry port and logistics hub on the Chinese border, that will then traverse the entire east-west breadth of Kazakhstan to reach the Caspian Sea oil port and city of Aktau, located on the Caspian eastern shore close to the Turkmenistan border.

The proposed second railroad is to link the city of Kashgar, at the western end of China's Xinjiang province, with Osh in southern Kyrgyzstan and nearby Andijan, an eastern Uzbek city on the southeastern edge of the fertile Ferghana Valley.

Chinese banks have been encouraged by Beijing to lend money to the countries that are part of the land-bridge, and Kazakhstan has become a major beneficiary of Chinese loans. Especially, Kazakhstan has been a major recipient of Chinese investment in Central Asian oil over the past two decades. In Congressional testimony in 2014, a U.S. policy adviser provided some of the specifics:

> China's largest national oil company, China National Petroleum Corporation (CNPC), is the majority owner of two of Kazakhstan's major oil companies (it owns 85.42 percent of Aktobe-MunaiGas and 67 percent of PetroKazakhstan) and is involved in several oil exploration and production projects throughout the country. The company also provides oilfield services in Kazakhstan and plans to build a refinery there. China's sovereign wealth fund, China Investment Corporation, also invested almost $1 billion in Kazakh energy in 2009.[1]

And from the Kazakhstan Side?

While it is evident that this growing partnership between Kazakhstan and China has created a "win-win" relationship, it is important to peer into what the Kazakh government is doing to translate these positive developments into better economic prospects for its citizens. There is no doubt that for the OBOR to make a significant dent in helping the Central Asian nations become economically stable—thus staving off political and terrorism-related instabilities—Kazakhstan should be the test case.

In geographical extent, Kazakhstan is the world's ninth largest country, spanning 2.7 million square kilometers. But it has a population of only 16 million, less than that of Florida (20 million). Vast stretches of this largely arid and semi-arid country have remained sparsely populated. Nonetheless, the concentration of economic activity in the eastern and western ends of Kazakhstan (as far apart as New York City and Salt Lake City) has led to the development of a workable transport infrastructure. Railroads and highways criss-cross the country; none are fully adequate, and many will become obsolete once the country begins to grow rapidly.

---

1. Testimony of Dennis C. Shea, Chairman, U.S.-China Economic and Security Review Commission, "China's Energy Engagement with Central Asia and Implications for the United States," for the hearing of the House Foreign Affairs Subcommittee on Europe, Eurasia, and Emerging Threats, on the subject of "The Development of Energy Resources in Central Asia," May 21, 2014.

The first container train pulls out of a logistics terminal jointly built by China and Kazakhstan in Lianyungang on China's Pacific Coast in February 2015. The rail line links Lianyungang and Almaty in Kazakhstan.

comprehensive infrastructure development plan. Kazakhstan's plan—announced by President Nursultan Nazarbayev in a State of the Nation address on November 11, 2014—is called the Nurly Zhol, or Lighted Path, an initiative directly tied in to OBOR. Kazakhstan had already proactively pitched its agenda toward China more than a decade earlier, and indeed Kazakhstan's pitch was one of the reasons Xi Jinping initially presented the OBOR plan in Astana, in October 2013.[2]

Unfolding the Nurly Zhol in his State of the Nation address, President Nursultan Nazarbayev made the following observations:

The Infrastructure Development Plan, which I want to make public today, will become the core of the New Economic Policy. It is intended to last for five years and is to run in parallel with the Second Five Year term of the Program of Accelerated Industrial and Innovative Development. More than 100 foreign companies intend to participate in its implementation. The total investment portfolio will amount to KZT6 trillion [about $18 billion at the December 2016 exchange rate between the U.S. dollar and Kazakh Tenge], with the state contributing 15% of the total. All the regions of Kazakhstan need to be closely connected by railroads, highways, and air services.... The New Economic Policy, "Nurly Zhol," will become a driver of growth in our economy during the coming years: 200,000 new jobs will be created by the construction of roads

The inadequacy of Kazakhstan's existing transport network poses a challenge to the OBOR. For instance, in 2011 China completed the corridor running from China's port of Lianyungang to Kazakhstan's Dostyk (Druzhba), and later, in 2012, to Khorgos. One nagging problem for these corridors, still unsolved, is the difference in railway gauges. While China uses a gauge of 1,435 millimeters, Kazakhstan, like all other former Soviet countries, uses the 1,520 millimeter gauge. At the China-Kazakhstan border crossings, passenger trains change bogies (the chassis under the wagon, on which the axles and wheels are mounted), while most freight is transferred to wagons with the wider gauge. Both methods require a good deal of heavy lifting equipment, and the trains must stop for 5 to 8 hours to complete the change of gauge.

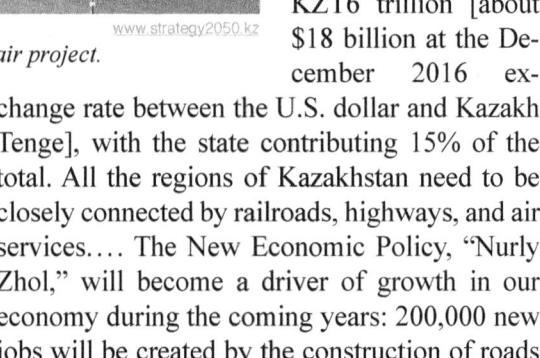

A Nurly Zhol road construction and repair project.

Breakout: 'Life Emerges Around Roads'

Recognizing the limitations of its rail and road infrastructure, the Kazakh government has proposed a

---

2. "China's One Belt, One Road Initiative and the Sino-Russian Entente: An Interview with Alexander Gabuev," Greg Shtraks, National Bureau of Asian Research, Aug. 9, 2016. http://www.nbr.org/research/activity.aspx?id=707

alone. And this means greater employment and growth of income for the population. "Nurly Zhol" will create a multiplier effect in other economic sectors: production of cement, metal, machinery, bitumen, equipment, and related services. Roads are lifelines for Kazakhstan. Life has always emerged and developed in our vast expanses around roads. Yet we must create a transport network such that car, railway, and airlines stretch in all directions from Astana.[3]

Xinhua

The Kazakh link of the Pan-Central Asia pipeline, here under construction in 2008.

Today, the integration of the Nurly Zhol and China's Silk Road Economic Belt is more than ever a matter of importance for Kazakhstan and Eurasia. When Kazakhstan's Foreign Minister Erlan Idrissov and Minister of Investment and Development Zhenis Kassymbek called a press conference on this subject on Nov. 30, 2016, it drew more than 80 representatives of foreign embassies and missions, including 50 ambassadors and heads of offices of international organizations. Idrissov said, according to the *Astana Times*, Dec. 1, 2016:

> Implementation of the Nurly Zhol program will ensure the connection of the Kazakh regions to intercontinental routes Western Kazakhstan-Western Europe [and] China-Iran, and will turn Kazakhstan into a major Eurasian transport and logistics hub that will connect the North with the South, the East with the West, the countries of the European Union, the Middle East and Southeast Asia.

Nuclear Fuel Fabrication

Beyond the transportation network, which Nurly Zhol addresses directly, Kazakhstan has immense mineral deposits of high quality. It is the world's leading uranium producer with 12% of world reserves and is the third largest chrome producer. Its deposits of copper and lead-zinc represent 10% and 13%, respectively, of world reserves. Kazakhstan is also well endowed with bauxite, coal, manganese, iron ore, phosphate, titanium, and tungsten. According to *Business Monitor* in 2013, its mining sector is set to grow to a value of almost $30 billion by 2017. However, except in the uranium sector, the government has not adequately addressed the development of this sector.

The development of Kazakhstan's uranium production, however, is impressive. From 2001 to 2015, production rose from 2,022 tons to about 23,800 tons per year (39% of world production), making Kazakhstan the world's leading uranium producer. Of its 17 mine projects, five are wholly owned by the government-owned Kazatomprom and 12 are joint ventures with foreign equity holders.[4]

Construction of a nuclear fuel fabrication plant—through a joint venture of Areva of France, Kazatomprom of Kazakhstan, and China General Nuclear Power Corporation (CGNPC)—was announced by the three companies on Dec. 6, 2016. France's Areva will provide the production technology, while most of the financing will come from CGNPC. Upon completion, the plant will be managed by a joint venture of Kazatomprom and CGNPC subsidiaries.

Kazakhstan Needs Nuclear Power

Notwithstanding the existing developments and plans for future developments, Kazakhstan lags in certain basic areas, resolution of which could help materi-

---

3. "Nurly Zhol, Bright Path to the Future: HE Nursultan A. Nazarbayev," *The Business Year*. https://www.thebusinessyear.com/kazakhstan-2015/nurly-zhol-bright-path-to-the-future/inside-perspective

4. "Uranium and Nuclear Power in Kazakhstan," World Nuclear Association, updated December 2016.

alize the country's economic prospects. *EIR*'s World Land-Bridge report[5] pointed out the importance of education and manpower development, as well as nuclear power generation for electricity and desalination of water to overcome dependence on surface water flow. These are necessary to attain well-rounded national development.

Although endowed with uranium, and soon to have a nuclear fuel fabrication plant, Kazakhstan does not have a single nuclear power plant. (A single Russian-built nuclear power reactor operated from 1972 to 1999, generating electricity and desalinating water.) Kazakhstan generates of about 13 GW of electrical power, of which about 81% comes from coal and the rest from natural gas. It imports some electricity from Russia and exports a small amount to Kyrgyzstan, another power-starved nation. The government has plans to enhance electricity generation. In 2012, the government's energy development plan called for at least a 60% increase in production by 2030, targeting an additional investment of close to $64 billion in this sector during that period.

Kazakhstan has plans for new nuclear power plants, but in November 2016, these plans were postponed because it was thought that there is no immediate need. But there *is* an immediate need: As with roads, life has always emerged and developed around cheap, abundant energy.

Kazakhstan must focus on water availability to enable its productive capabilities and to improve living conditions at the household level. Almost 90% of the country is considered arid or semi-arid, with low humidity. In terms of water resources, the country is among those at the low end of the scale in Eurasia. Kazakhstan's average annual surface water is 100.5 cubic kilometers (km^3), of which 56.5 km^3 is from precipitation within the country; the rest comes from China, Uzbekistan, Kyrgyzstan, and Russia. Surface water resources are also very unevenly distributed.[6]

Although water is a major hurdle for Kazakhstan, desalination of water from the Caspian Sea could fully alleviate water shortages in the north, west, and parts of the south. Here again, nuclear power would help.

---

5. *The New Silk Road Becomes the World Land-Bridge*, Executive Intelligence Review, November 2014.

6. T.T. Sarsenbekov and S.K. Ahmetov, "Report on the Regional Water Partnership (Republic of Kazakhstan)," Global Water Partnership. http://www.gwp.org/Global/GWP-CACENA_Files/en/pdf/kazakhstan.pdf

Every Day Counts In Today's Showdown To Save Civilization

That's why you need EIR's **Daily Alert Service**, a strategic overview compiled with the input of Lyndon LaRouche, and delivered to your email 5 days a week.

The election of Donald Trump to the Presidency of the Untied States has launched a new global era whose character has yet to be determined. The Obama-Clinton drive toward confrontation with Russia has been disrupted--but what will come next?

Over the next weeks and months there will be a pitched battle to determine the course of the Trump Administration. Will it pursue policies of cooperation with Russia and China in the New Silk Road, as the President-Elect has given some signs of? Will it follow through against Wall Street with Glass-Steagall?

The opposition to these policies will be fierce. If there is to be a positive outcome to this battle, an informed citizenry must do its part--intervening, educating, inspiring. That's why you need the EIR Daily Alert more than ever.

TUESDAY, NOVEMBER 22, 2016

Volume 3, Number 65

EIR Daily Alert Service

P.O. Box 17390, Washington, DC 20041-0390

- Only Global Solutions, Based on New Principles, Can Work
- Tulsi Gabbard Meets with Donald Trump Regarding Syria
- Robert Kagan Throws in the Towel, Complains U.S. Is Becoming 'Solipsistic'
- War Party Moving To Preempt Trump-Putin Reset
- Syrian Army Makes More Progress in Aleppo
- Duterte Gives OK to Nuclear Power for Philippines
- Europe Will Suffer from Maintaining Russia Sanctions
- Former Chilean Diplomat Confirmed, 'We Will Joyfully Welcome Xi Jinping'
- Duterte and Putin Establish Philippines-Russia Cooperation
- François Fillon, Pro-Russian Thatcherite, Wins First Round of French Right-Wing Presidential Primary

EDITORIAL

Only Global Solutions, Based on New Principles, Can Work

III. The End of the EU Empire

Italian Citizens Defend Their Constitution

Elke Fimmen of the **Bürgerrechtsbewegung Solidarität** (BüSo), *the German political party founded and led by Helga Zepp-LaRouche, interviewed Liliana Gorini, chairwoman of* Movisol, *on Dec. 6.*

Elke Fimmen: Good evening. My name is Elke Fimmen. Today I am speaking with Liliana Gorini in Milan about the failure of the constitutional referendum in Italy on Sunday, Dec. 4. Liliana is the chairwoman of the Movement for Civil Rights and Solidarity—Movisol—the *BüSo's* sister organization in Italy.

To many, the outcome of the referendum was seen as the third shocking revolt against an Establishment which doesn't care about its citizens—following the Brexit vote in Great Britain and the election of Donald Trump in the United States. The EU finance ministers downplayed the result, saying it represents no danger to the Euro system, that everything is under control. That is obviously not the case, because the banking system throughout Europe and in the transatlantic sector as a whole is totally bankrupt. Just today the Italian bank Monte dei Paschi di Siena announced that it had triggered the first phase of a partial "bail-in" and on December 31 would convert a billion euros of so-called "subordinated" bonds into bank stock. That is supposed to save Monte dei Paschi. The situation is thus highly unstable, with poten-

Italian voters soundly defeated Prime Minister Renzi's constitutional reform.

wikimedia commons

tially dramatic results for all of Europe.

Hello, Liliana.

Liliana Gorini: Good evening.

Fimmen: You said before the vote that it would turn out to be 60-40 percent against the referendum, i.e. against Prime Minister Renzi's proposed changes in the constitution. So first of all, congratulations on the success of your forecast.

Gorini: (laughing) Yes, that is the first time that I've been so accurate, and I am very happy that it happened that way, but I was rather sure it would, because the Italians have had their fill of austerity measures. They saw that Renzi's proposal accepted all this austerity and cutbacks, and above all, they saw the Constitution as a defense of Italy's sovereignty. For example, there are several articles in the constitution which amount to a precise defense of labor and of citizens' savings. And for this reason, JP Morgan had wanted the Italian constitution set aside—and not only the Italian constitution; these bankers wanted to get rid of all constitutions, especially those which were born out of opposition to fascism.

Fimmen: Yes, that also answers the question as to why this referendum went the way it did, and why so many citizens—almost 70 percent of the electorate resident in Italy— participated in the election, and then voted against the proposal so decisively. It's actually unusual for people to be able to see right off the bat the reality behind such questions—and I've also seen the ballot—questions which are presented rather deceptively, claiming that they will simplify everything, lower expenditures, and do various other things which they won't do. Therefore you have to say that the Italians have voted very intelligently.

Gorini: it's true that this was a good indication of Italians' intelligence, because the issue was really deceptive—the Five-Star Party had petitioned the constitutional court to invalidate that deceptive question, which it didn't do; the propaganda of the Renzi government, which sent out the ballot with a letter from Renzi to all Italians living abroad—there are four million such voters—was unbelievable, and was totally against the law. And it was obviously deceptive: for instance, it claimed it would abolish the Senate, but actually, it would have kept the Senate while ending the election of the Senate by the voters.

The constitutional changes would have also abolished the National Council for Economics and Labor (CNEL), a typical free market measure, since this was one of those institutions which should actually define investment policy; this measure would also be a lead-in to the European Union's exercising more power over Italy.

The result was thanks to the efforts of various movements—including Movisol, which campaigned for a "no," and the Five-Star Party. For example, I attended a conference in Alba on banking separation, Glass-Steagall, on November 12; I spoke with a parliamentarian of the Five-Star Party who afterwards, with her colleagues, launched a last-ditch rail campaign, i.e. they went throughout all Italy on trains, and explained to the people, one after another, why the Constitution is so important, and how national sovereignty would be abolished under the change. That was very important. Thus the campaign for a "no" was important because the propaganda was totally opaque.

Renzi has obviously promised much that he could not deliver, and the people voted against Renzi's lies. This vote was not, as Merkel said—I heard her interview with the German ARD station today—an internal matter; it was a referendum against the European Union's dictatorship. One woman said this outright in response to an exit-poll. I heard the various questions which were asked, and she said, I voted "no" because I want to retain my sovereignty.

Xinhua/Jin Yu

Senators vote for the 2017 budget in Rome, Italy, on Dec. 7, 2016, giving final approval and clearing the way for the announced resignation of Prime Minister Matteo Renzi.

Fimmen: That is really a really important process—that the population understands what it's all about; and I have read that there was one—surely more—but one prominent constitutional expert, Prof. Caracciolo, who showed that at least four articles of the new constitution would place EU law on the same level as constitutional law. And, as you said, this would explicitly be a prelude to achieving the goal of this constitutional change—with, I believe, 47 changes in the constitution—which changes would "profoundly streamline the multi-faceted system of governance between the EU, the Italian state, and local autonomous institutions." And thus it would really effectively degrade the parliament into purely an executive organ for Brussels; and thus it's very important that it has been thrown out.

But you also spoke about the lies, and said that the

population simply didn't believe any more that there should now be "great reforms" like what has already been carried out in Italy over recent years through EU policies, through the rescue of the banks—policies which Renzi never really questioned. He had had something of a showdown with the EU over the budget, but that was not really effective in defending Italy. Or, how do you see it?

Gorini: Yes, that's true. And so people could not believe in this confrontation between Renzi, and Juncker and the European Union, because during the three years he's been Prime Minister, they have seen that he actually has carried out all the EU's diktats.

Just today, a study by Italy's statistics agency ISTAT, reported that one fourth of the Italian population lives in poverty. The cutbacks, especially in health care, are dreadful, and I know this from personal experience, because I have also had medical problems. Everything is either paid for privately, or not at all, and there are cutbacks everywhere. People saw Renzi's whole campaign—also on the earthquakes, where he said he wanted to defend the schools, and that they would be rebuilt—as election propaganda, and nobody believed it. Renzi went around the earthquake regions in his private helicopter, and people don't believe him any more after three years. You must realize that Italy has practically received the "Greek treatment" from the European Union. And for two years Renzi has made fun of Greece. So no one believes him.

Fimmen: That—along with his embrace of Obama and Merkel recently, when Obama once again came to Europe—surely hasn't contributed to people seeing him as a potentially independent figure, and that is obviously a real problem.

The question is, what will happen now? Because the Italian president at first refused to let Renzi resign, saying that he should remain in office to get the budget adopted. But there are also these fundamental questions about the budget: What is the state of Italy's sovereignty? Can you really invest? Can you do something which is useful for the country? Or can you only bow to the EU's diktat? And the question is, what are Italy's options for bestirring itself and creating new maneuvering room? How do you see this?

Gorini: Yes, this is obviously difficult now, because Mattarella, the President, has actually frozen Renzi's resignation until the budget has been decided on, and it must obviously move very quickly—tomorrow, for ex-

ample, it will be debated in the Senate, and then in the Chamber of Deputies. The idea is that it must be voted on by Christmas and be finished with, and then another government will take over until there are new elections. But the "no" front is against this; they want new elections and early elections, as quickly as possible—that is, the Five-Star Party and the Lega Nord want new elections.

And it seems that Renzi does, too. He has not resigned as chairman of the Democratic Party, and apparently he also wants new elections, because he thinks that his career is still not over; he thinks that he has 40% (laughing) of the vote, which is ridiculous, because most of the people who voted "yes" were not Democratic Party voters. They were people who feared that either the Lega Nord or the Five-Star Party could come into the government, and they especially were afraid of the warning from the *Financial Times*, which wrote before the elections that if the "no" won, eight banks would collapse. That was a typical Mafioso threat from the City of London.

But it will surely take a while; new elections will apparently occur in March or April. And in the meantime we will campaign; I have already written an editorial, a declaration, in which, as head of Movisol, I clarify the key points for a new government.

The Five-Star Party is also currently debating what its government program should be, which it has not yet determined. They have the potential to actually become the government, and they would like to emerge as the ruling party. And therefore, we have asked all our contacts in the Five-Star Party to make banking separation—which they also have introduced into parliament—the first plank of this government program, because, as everyone says, the fate of Monte dei Paschi di Siena and the bank emergency must be the first point of action. And without banking separation, all the debts which come from derivatives, will be shifted onto the shoulders of the citizens through bail-in, or through bailout by the state. In either case the citizens will pay the tab.

The Fundamental Change on the Agenda

Fimmen: Yes, precisely. That is, I think, absolutely crucial, and also links the situation in Italy with that of the other European countries—obviously also that in the United States, where there is a huge debate and the possibility of putting through Glass-Steagall. But also in Germany, where Glass-Steagall must absolutely be

wikimedia commons/Armin Kübelbeck

German Finance Minister Wolfgang Schäuble

put on the agenda, because we have—with Deutsche Bank, the bank which is entangled with the most derivatives in history—a really huge elephant in the room.

This need to actually implement a fundamental reform—not a pseudo-reform and not just any phony measures—is now really on the agenda, and I think that the many proposed laws for Glass-Steagall, for banking separation, which exist in Italy, due primarily to Movisol's initiative, are now obviously totally crucial.

The whole financial system is totally linked and entangled together. That also explains the hysteria of people like (German Finance Minister) Wolfgang Schäuble, who meddled inappropriately in the Italian vote. He said the Italians should vote "yes"; but now, following the recent EU Finance Ministers' summit, he was one of those who downplayed everything, and said, "No, no, no reason for panic; there is no danger for the Euro; it is all under control, and you can proceed as before."

This only shows the degree of hysteria, because the old paradigm is really ending, and thus I believe we are really coming to a point very soon at which this fundamental reorganization is absolutely on the agenda.

Can you say something in this connection about the other measures which Movisol advocates, such as collaboration with the Silk Road, with Russia, and also the development of Africa, since the refugee issue really represents a very acute problem for you in Italy?

Gorini: Yes, sure. That is our "four points." We have a short program similar to Lyndon LaRouche's "four laws," an emergency program for the government. That, first of all, calls for bank separation, which is the most urgent, due to Monte dei Paschi. And you're right that you have to do the same with Deutsche Bank, as Helga Zepp-La-Rouche and Lyndon LaRouche have proposed: first, Glass-Steagall, and then secure the accounts of these banks, but only if you have first done away with the derivatives.

The second point is obviously the reconstruction of the earthquake regions, and the point is also that the European Union's diktat cannot be accepted. Because the EU has opposed the budget, and demands that these schools and new buildings not be built according to anti-earthquake standards. That is really criminal. They want hundreds more people to die. That is the second point.

Then, cooperation with the Silk Road and Russia, and the immediate abrogation of the sanctions against Russia, which Renzi actually had proposed at the beginning. But then, at the meeting in Berlin with Merkel and Obama, he retreated on this point, and accepted the sanctions. That must be reversed; sanctions not only destroy the German economy, but also our industry, and especially agriculture in northern Italy. And the people—industrialists, and small and medium-sized firms—are really very enraged at Renzi on this point as well.

And the fourth point is, in Italy's case, investment in science and culture. Because culture is very important in our country, and Renzi has made huge cutbacks.

Fimmen: Yes, I think we have now discussed a few things, and now our viewers should have a better understanding, and more in depth, of what this referendum was really about, and why it was an important milestone in burying the old paradigm, and creating a new era of reconstruction, the construction of the real economy, and an actual future again; and absolutely exploiting this opportunity.

Liliana, thank you very much for this interview, and I hope that we will have the opportunity to speak again soon.

Gorini: My pleasure, and all the best to you. Keep it up!

Translated from German.

The EU Is a Dead Man Walking

by Claudio Celani

Dec. 12—The reaction of EU institutions to the Italian constitutional referendum (see *EIR* No. 50) can be described as "Hitler in the bunker." The EU is a dead proposition, after the Brexit, the U.S. elections and the events that have left Angela Merkel as the only survivor—for the time being—of leading EU heads of government in the last weeks. However, the EU Commission, the European Central Bank (ECB), and the German government itself are refusing to surrender, and keep pushing their agenda. It will end like 1945—hopefully including a Nuremberg trial!

As the Italian voters rejected a constitutional change 60 to 40 which would have enslaved the country to the EU dictatorial regime, the EU response was: "It was not about the EU; it was a domestic Italian affair." However, new war plans were drafted and announced against Italy. They moved to plunge Italy into a banking crisis and force it to submit to a Greece-like Troika regime.

Italy does have an urgent banking crisis to solve, but this must be seen on the backdrop of the general crisis of the trans-Atlantic banking system, which is hopelessly bankrupt, and cannot be solved if the issue of commercial banking versus speculative banking is not addressed.

In fact, the Italian banking crisis is mainly due to huge credit losses, whereas the rest of the trans- Atlantic system is burdened by trillions of unpayable financial assets. Additionally, the Italian crisis would be under control if the government were free to use its sovereign power. Instead, it is forbidden by EU laws to bail out a troubled bank unless it first plunders the bank's depositors through so-called "bail-in" regulations. And even after having plundered depositors, Italy is not allowed to recapitalize banks with taxpayers' money, because this would "unbalance" the budget! The only measure offered by the EU to Italy is to take a loan from an EU fund, attached to brutal austerity conditions and to direct EU management of government accounts.

It is exactly this policy that voters rejected in the Dec. 4 referendum.

In defiance of those voters, two days after the vote, Volker Wieland, a member of the so-called "Economic Wise Men's" advisory board to the German government, gave an interview to the *Handelsblatt* economic daily in which he said that Italy should go to the European Stability Mechanism (ESM), and also get the IMF "involved in the aid program." The ESM is a fund set up by the EU to loan money to financially troubled governments, conditional on brutal austerity measures implemented by a caretaker committee called "the Troika," composed by representatives of the ESM itself, the IMF and the European Central Bank.

The plan, Wieland said, "on one side would represent a 'shield' in case of a debt crisis in Italy, and on the other side, the ESM and IMF together could apply the right pressure to unblock reforms."

How insane the Troika regime is, has been shown in recent years in the case of Greece. Greece was put under the Troika regime in 2011, and since then the national economy has collapsed, unemployment and poverty have sky-

wikimedia commons

A greatly inflated symbol of the bankrupt euro, in Frankfurt, with the equally bankrupt Deutsche Bank headquarters in the background.

rocketed, and the country's foreign debt has increased.

EU statistics show that official unemployment in Greece has grown from 12.7% to 24.9%, GDP per capita has plunged from 20,300 to 17,000, poverty-stricken families have increased from 27.7% to 35.7%, and the debt-to-GDP ratio has increased from 146.2% to 176.9%.

Such figures are the result of the EU-imposed target of a 3.5% primary budget surplus for Greece, something impossible to achieve. A primary surplus, or deficit, is the balance of income and expenditures of the government before interest payments. This surplus should then be used, according to the Troika, to pay back foreign debt. Only a few among EU countries have achieved a primary surplus in the last decades, and the strongest country, Germany, reached at best slightly above 2%. Thus, insisting on a 3.5% target for Greece is sheer insanity and an intention of genocide.

This was confirmed at the last meeting of the Eurogroup of Finance Ministers on Dec. 7, where Greece was denied short-term measures for debt reduction because the 3.5% target has not been achieved!

Not that things in Italy have been better; as a matter of fact, Italy has self-imposed an austerity therapy since 2011, when an ECB-led coup installed a technocratic government led by Mario Monti, and Italy signed up to commitments for "reforms" that amount to an "automatic pilot," as ECB head Mario Draghi declared in 2013.

Italy has been an EU champion in consistent primary budget surplus, but this is not enough blood for the EU, and a Troika regime would presumably set the same targets for Italy as for Greece.

The explanation for this genocidal approach is that the Troika bailout programs are in reality schemes for bank bailouts. In fact, most of the €220 billions received by Greece under the ESM program and its predecessor, the European Financial Stability Facility (EFSF) fund, never reached Greece, but were used to pay Greece's international creditors, with German and French banks at the front of the line.

In the case of Italy, it is feared that the failure of a systemic bank such as Monte dei Paschi di Siena (MPS), the most troubled financial institution in Italy, would unleash a systemic collapse. It is also feared that a government refusal to implement a bail-in scheme, would set a precedent which goes against the very foundations of the trans-Atlantic system, which sets the "stability of the system" as the priority over the protection of deposits.

Thus, after the warning by Merkel's advisor Wieland, other orders were issued from the bunker.

On Dec. 7, Moody's rating agency changed the outlook for Italy from "stable" to "negative." Although this is not yet a rating cut, it does have an effect on Italy's financial stability. Rating agencies have regularly determined runs on Italian bonds by lowering their ratings in previous years. This is typical of tactics used to blackmail Italy into accepting mafia-style "protection" by the ECB, in exchange for surrender to austerity programs and technocratic governments.

The next steps were taken by the ECB. First, on Dec. 8, the ECB Governing Board decided to give a clear signal that it intends to continue the life-support measures for the bankrupt system, called Quantitative Easing (QE), indefinitely into the future. The ECB extended QE for six months beyond the planned deadline of March 2017, but said that it could extend it further at will. It then reduced from 80 to 60 billion Euros the amount of assets purchased monthly from banks, which led some commentators to speak of an initial tapering of QE. However, the ECB had already reduced its purchases to 60 billion in the last months, because there are not enough eligible assets on the market. Indeed, the ECB also announced that it has expanded the range of eligible assets, including one-year maturities.

Even the German daily *Der Spiegel* commented that the ECB money will only go to inflate the stock market and the real estate bubble, and warned that all such bubbles in the past, from the Tulip Bubble to the subprime bubble, always ended in a crash.

After having promised an additional half trillion euros for speculators in the next twelve months, the ECB then turned down a request from Monte dei Paschi (MPS) to have an additional 30 days time to find €5bn to recapitalize itself! This dramatically worsened the Italian banking crisis, as it is mathematically impossible that MPS could find the money by the established deadline of Dec. 31. With this move, the ECB intended to put the Italian government, already in the middle of a crisis because of Prime Minister Renzi's resignation, into a corner, and force it accede to a bail-in/Troika combination.

Enter Glass-Steagall

However, a major defection took place in the banking establishment. Jens Weidmann, head of the German central bank (Bundesbank), stated in an interview with Reuters Dec. 12 that in a special circumstance such as

Banca Monte dei Paschi di Siena in Pisa.

creative commons/Petar Milsevic

the Italian case, a violation of European bail-in rules could be accepted.

Clearly, Weidmann is worried about the effects of an MPS default on Germany's large zombie bank, Deutsche Bank. His statement, however, puts the issue of depositors' protection up-front. In Italy, Weidmann says, "high-risk financial products were apparently sold to people who were actually looking for more conservative products. If now, for political reasons, you want to protect investors who are considered to need special protection, this could occur for instance in the framework of targeted state transfers."

Weidmann was referring to tens of thousands of MPS customers who were lured into purchasing up to €2 billion of subordinated bonds, and who in case of a bail-in would see all their money wiped out. The Italian government is already considering excluding those customers from a bail-in of MPS, as part of a government recapitalization with taxpayers' money. An executive order has already been drafted, and will be implemented in case the planned "market solution" for MPS fails before the Dec. 31 deadline, as it looks probable that it will.

The issue of depositors' protection is the central issue addressed by the Glass-Steagall Act, which the LaRouche organization is pushing worldwide. In the case of MPS, it is urgent that the government intervene

to guarantee deposits, but also credits to the real economy. The rest of the assets side of the bank, instead, must be sorted out, and all assets which cannot be priced must be cancelled. This is a reversal of the approach adopted by EU regulations and by the Dodd-Frank bill in the U.S.A. Such "reforms," in fact, have only focused on the bank-lending side, totally neglecting the derivatives and other fluff on the banks' balance sheets.

These bank assets have prices which are determined by bank "internal models," and do not correspond to reality. Instead of sorting out this mess, EU and U.S. regulations have imposed capital requirements related to so-called risk-weighted assets, which include loans, but leave out derivatives whose risk is not weighted. Thus, those banks which lend more to the real economy are disadvantaged in comparison with banks with an overblown derivative portfolio.

The Italian banking system has been targeted by the ECB because it has accumulated between 200 and 400 billions of Non-Performing Loans (NPL). Most of these loans are credits to large, small, and medium enterprises and farms, and mortgage loans to families. Ever since the Italian economy plunged into a depression in 2008, and has never recovered because of the "primary surplus" regime, those credits have become foul. At least eight major banks are in a troubled situation and need a recapitalization under EU guidelines.

The case of MPS is special because it involves both NPLs and derivatives, i.e. commercial and speculative losses. MPS is reported to have €47bn of NPLs, which the bank has covered with only 20bn special reserves. But the root of MPS' troubles lies in the so-called strategy of "inorganic expansion" in financial trading, which MPS started in 1995, when Glass-Steagall-like regulations were lifted in Italy. This "inorganic expansion" culminated, as an investigating committee of the Tuscany Regional Council has established, with the insane acquisition of Antonveneta Bank from Santander in 2008, which has cost MPS a total of €18 billion. In order to cover such losses on the balance sheet, the MPS management eventually bought derivatives from Deutsche Bank and Nomura which produced more losses.

The acquisition of Antonveneta at three times its market value made no sense from a commercial or financial standpoint, but was a "systemic" operation to bai lout Santander, one of the largest European systemic banks. As evidence of the nature of the operation, which was authorized by the Italian central bank under Mario Draghi, MPS head Giuseppe Mussari was eventually appointed as head of the Italian Banking Association.

Thus, an urgent intervention into MPS and all other Italian banks must involve a mechanism that: 1. replaces the current, corrupt management, with public officials with both competence and proven integrity; 2. immediately recapitalizes the bank with government money in order to protect depositors and savers, and prevent a run on the bank; 3. creates a committee that sorts out the bank assets, protecting commercial loans but canceling all assets which are not salable. In doing this, the Italian government shall act in full sovereignty, without asking EU institutions or EU member governments.

This will precipitate a crisis in the trans-Atlantic financial system, but a welcome one. Financial measures, however, are not sufficient to turn the situation around. The Italian economy needs an urgent physical recovery, otherwise banks will keep producing losses. Therefore, the second step must be a national recovery program with large-scale infrastructure investments.

Whether the new Italian government led by former Foreign Minister Paolo Gentiloni will take those steps is questionable. Gentiloni is a member of an old aristocratic family with a long tradition in modern politics. The characteristic of this species is that they keep their feet in all shoes, ready to play the winning game. Gentiloni's grandfather, Count of the Holy Roman Empire Vincenzo Ottorino Gentiloni, was a co-founder of the Italian Liberal Party in 1912, and brokered a deal with the Vatican in 1913, to have Catholics vote

wikimedia

Paolo Gentiloni, Matteo Renzi's replacement as prime minister, announcing the formation of his cabinet, December 12, 2016.

for the new party. This had two consequences: it paved the way for a government that led Italy into WWI in 1915, shifting from the alliance with Germany and Austria to an alliance with France and Britain; and it sabotaged the process then underway to create a Christian Democratic Party based on anti-oligarchical principles.

Grandson Paolo started his career as a student member of Potere Operaio, a left-wing radical group one step away from terrorism. He then became an environmentalist, and finally a member of the liberal wing of the Democratic Party. As a Foreign Minister he went along with EU and NATO decisions, while at the same time keeping up a dialogue with Russia on Libya and Mediterranean issues.

Gentiloni received a mandate from President Sergio Mattarella to run the government until a new election law is ready, and then go to early elections. This sets a life expectancy of a few months, but events could change it, and even extend it to the natural end of the legislature next year. In the mean time, his cabinet, which won't substantially change from the previous Renzi government, must deal with the banking crisis and other emergencies, such as earthquake reconstruction, as well as fighting with the EU on the budget.

From the government's moves on MPS in the coming days, we will know whether the government has minimally learned the lesson of the Dec. 4 vote.

LaRouche's *Fourth Law*: Hamilton and Einstein

by Philip Rubinstein

The following is an edited transcript of a class given on November 23, 2016, by Manhattan Project leader Philip Rubinstein.

What I want to do is to, in part, talk about this question of Lyndon LaRouche's Four Laws—really Hamilton, but also not just Hamilton, but rather Hamilton in the context of the Fourth of LaRouche's Laws. I'm going to read just a little bit of the Fourth Law, which is Lyndon LaRouche's expansion of Hamilton. We should be fairly clear on some things. Hamilton has a whole lot on the productivity of labor. In this sense, we will also discuss *what LaRouche adds to the productivity of labor.* Because what LaRouche cites as the fourth principle, the Fourth Law, is not simply in Hamilton. It goes further.

First: From Hamilton

Hamilton talks about the increase of the productivity of labor; of course his *Report On Manufactures* is a lengthy discourse on the importance of manufacturing from the standpoint of the improvement of the productivity of labor. Essentially, the reason he gives for manufacturing and the importance of manufacturing, the underlying principal, you could say, is the increase of the productivity of labor.

Hamilton cites, through machinery for instance, "It is now proper to proceed a step further, and enumerate the principal cir-

creative commons

Bust of Alexander Hamilton by Franklin Simmons, 1906.

cumstances from which it may be inferred that manufacturing establishments not only occasion a positive augmentation of the produce and revenue of society, but that they contribute to rendering them greater than they could possibly be without such establishments." These circumstances are: (here's a shocker for you) the division of labor! I think a lot of people have a problem with that, that indeed the *division of labor* is an advantage in productivity, particularly if it's done properly.

Secondly, the *extension of the use of machinery*—obviously the ability to expand labor, and as he goes on later, to expand the productivity of labor; the addition of a class of the community not normally engaged in productivity; the promotion of immigration from foreign countries; furnishing a greater scope for talents which discriminate men from each other; the affording of more ample and various fields for enterprise, and so on. The main point I want to make is that he started out with the division of labor and the extension of machinery.

It's very clear otherwise that the point he makes about manufacturing, "the foregoing suggestions are not designed to inculcate an opinion that manufacturing industry is more productive than that of agriculture. They are intended rather to show that the reverse of the proposition is not ascertained." He says that people are saying that agriculture is productive and manufacturing is not. His argument is that manufacturing of course is indeed productive, and that, ultimately, it increases productivity, "and from these causes united the mere separation of that of the cultivator from that of the artificer has the effect of augmenting the productive powers of labor." The point is it augments the productive powers of labor. In a sense, that is the whole point of the longest of Hamilton's reports. *The Report on Manufactures* is far and away the longest one.

The one point I want to make, a rather large point, before I cite one particular point from LaRouche, is, if you look at the *Report on Public Credit*, if you look at the *Constitutionality of the National Bank*, then, of course, there's the *Report on the National Bank*, they all have a certain principle which you find in the Federalist from the very beginning. This is why Hamilton is often accused of being an authoritarian, a monarchist, a totalitarian, because, in every one of these, he starts from the standpoint that the Union, as it's called later, during the Civil War, the nation as a whole, comes first. That comes before the states, in particular.

This is very clear in the argument on the *Constitutionality of the National Bank*. Because what is it that Thomas Jefferson and Attorney General Edmund Randolph argue in particular? Their main argument is that the Federal Government does not have the enumerated powers to create a corporation, not just a bank, any corporation; that it has no right to create a corporation that has a legal identity. That's their big argument. Then who has that right? The states! The states have a right to create corporations, and indeed, the Federal Government creating corporations interferes with the laws of the state. Almost the entirety of Hamilton's argument for the constitutionality of the National Bank is that the states do not have any right that conflicts with the right of the Federal Government. Of course the Federal Government has the right to override the laws of states.

What is the reason he gives for this? Sovereignty in part, yes, but it is basically the "General Welfare" clause. What is the object of the Federal Government? The Federal Government has the power to enact everything that it deems necessary to achieve its appropriate object. In fact, it is interesting to see how much these were the arguments that occurred. I don't think the average candidate today could engage in the discussion. Their vocabulary is too limited. Hamilton asked: What is the object of the Federal Government? The welfare,

the general welfare of the population; the general welfare of the country as a whole. Therefore, the National Bank, the right to incorporate the National Bank is not only Constitutional, it is necessary.

One of the arguments that goes on, and you'll see it if you read it, which is part of the value of reading it, is that Jefferson and Randolph—and you can see that this already is a southern split—Jefferson and Randolph want to say that the word "necessary," which is in the Constitution, means only such things as are "absolutely necessary." Hamilton says: Wait a minute; necessary doesn't mean only those things which are absolutely necessary. In fact, it means quite the opposite: whatever you need to achieve the object of the Federal Government. So these are very important, but also very serious documents. The *Federalist Papers* of course opens up with the assertion that the Union has to come above the states.

Einstein and the Human Identity

Today, what we have is an opportunity. To look at LaRouche's recent Sunday discussion, was he recommending that we apply Einstein's principle to our discussion with somebody in the Trump cabinet? Maybe, but I think he was getting at something a little bit different, which is, how do we approach the entire situation? Are we out to simply win somebody to our side, to count up the score on the cabinet or in the Congress or whatever?

No, he is saying you have to have the same view that somebody like Einstein had; that, for Einstein, it was not a matter of the mathematics, per se. There is a lot of confusion on this. It's not that Einstein didn't use mathematics, but the mathematics was not the reality. That is something we can discuss at another time, because Einstein's view, in his debate with people like Niels Bohr and Werner Heisenberg, the explicit debate was, essentially, do we know reality? It wasn't things like, "is it waves or is it particles"—that is part of the debate; it is not unimportant, not something to overlook, but, the real debate between them was that you had (what we at a certain point called a positivist orientation), a very sharp denial that we do know reality, by people like Heisenberg, Max Born, Bohr in particular, because they were the ones who carried out the debate with Einstein to a large extent.

Einstein's point was: No, it's not just that "God doesn't play dice." That was the clever phrase, you

Albert Einstein, by Doris Ulmann

creative commons

more was in it than we thought. I find these things fascinating—there was an estimate at one point that there were about 200 billion galaxies. This was based on scanning, because we can only look at so much of the universe; telescopes have certain angles of observation and so forth. Now given the fact that we have an increased data base, which is actually going to be expanding a great deal more over the next 4 or 5 years, the estimate now is that we have 2 trillion galaxies. Two trillion galaxies! Now if you think that it is believed that the average galaxy has between 100 and 200 billion stars....you realize that there is something like 10^{23}, possibly, stars. That's a big number.

Cognition, Productivity and the Universe

Now, think of the following, because part of what LaRouche is getting at, and this—we only have one access to this—is that *the universe actually develops*. It is not just a general idea. There is a real development somehow in the universe. As Vernadsky puts it, and LaRouche has referred to Vernadsky, there is a multiply-connected reality between the *abiotic*, the *biotic* and the *cognitive*. Now, for the most part, how do we think about it? We think the abiotic, somehow develops into the biotic, and the biotic develops into the cognitive. Now in one sense, in terms of time, at least in terms of the human species, something like that seems to have gone on. If you look at the human body, it carries the human mind. The human mind is somehow located where the body is, at one level. But the truth of the matter is, that the governing principle of the development of the universe is a cognitive, or at least analogous to a cognitive, process—that the way we discover things, and I think the way we act when we are actually discovering being creative, is the way the universe itself develops. Then it's also the other way around. There is a cognitive principle, or a principle of development like human cognition, and that human cognition develops the universe.

In other words, the universe produced us so it could develop further. The universe produces a capability for creativity, so that the universe can change, develop, expand, but expand in some direction toward further existence of cognition, toward discoveries. You have to realize that when we discover a physical principle and

could say that was a soundbite, but that wasn't all that Einstein meant. He meant: No, there is a reality. We're not talking about the fact that things come into existence when we observe them and go out of existence when we don't observe them. There is something real called the universe, and Einstein's work was about the nature of that universe.

I think what one has to reflect on is our whole conception, and LaRouche does allude to this in the discussion with the "Basement" (LaRouche PAC Science Team)—our whole conception of a universe, a universe that is developing, a universe that is changing, that this essentially rests on Einstein's work in special and general relativity. Up to the 1920s there was no such thing as really a theory of the cosmos. It was just there. In fact there wasn't that much there. It wasn't nearly as big. We found it was a lot bigger than we thought it was, a lot utilize it, we are not taking nature and using nature, so to speak. *We are changing nature.* Because what we do does not occur naturally, except for the intervention of human beings. You take nuclear fission, you take electricity in the form that we use it—these things don't grow on trees! You don't walk out and pick an electric wire off your tree, plug it into your house and light up your wife or husband as the case may be.

These things are actual changes. We basically have the possibility, as we work on the subatomic scale, of using such things as the differences in spin, that is angular momentum of the object itself, other sorts of issues, (even though a lot of the science that is involved in this right now is strange epistemologically and methodologically), there are certain things we've learned to deal with. With the improvement in the methodological outlook, we could begin to use these things in an entirely different way. One point LaRouche made today is: You take Einstein's work on relativity theory—we don't really know how all this works. And, by the way, Einstein himself did not consider general relativity to be complete. He considered it, not that it was an unfinished project—his project, you might say was finished—but the theory was not a complete theory about the organization of the universe, even from the standpoint of gravitational force. We don't know the distribution of matter, we don't know some of the other aspects of the gravitational field, and so on and so forth.

We have to recognize that what Einstein did discover, so to speak, is the fact that the universe that we live in is dominated by, and I mean this literally, we are talking about what amounts to a gravitational field or an electromagnetic field. These things govern the way we exist in the solar system, it gives us clues as to the way we have to look at galactic process, and we have to take this whole thing a great deal further, but these are the kinds of changes that we need to make. What we need is an entire change in our outlook on the process of discovering what is in the universe and that this is the nature of mankind. I'm sure LaRouche may have more to say about these things, but at least on one basic level, the question is: Do we understand what it means to say that the nature of mankind is creative discovery—by that I mean that for each individual human being, that is his or her identity.

Now, what is human identity? The fact is there is a universal human identity. This I think is a great deal of the point LaRouche is getting across. Our identity is

that human beings are capable of adding to, communicating and making actual discoveries of principle and being part of a process. For example, if you were part of the space program, it wasn't just, "Okay, we're going to the Moon." It was part of a unified conception, that the United States—yes it was a race with the Soviet Union—but fundamentally we were out to discover the nature of the solar system. We even had a President who said that in his speech. There is the famous point, if you listen to the whole speech, that goes beyond that we are going to the Moon, where President Kennedy talks about going throughout the solar system, other planets, and so on and so forth. The idea was then we had a mission as a nation, but also as part of the planet as a whole, to make a voyage of discovery.

Indeed you had this strange kind of event, because you had the all the Apollo projects, and that stopped. Then there was sort of no space program, and one day you wake up and find that Voyager has gone another couple of zillion miles, and suddenly there was a spurt of something of a space program, and then it would die out again, and then you would find that Voyager went a little further five years later, and so on and so forth. But the idea, that for every human individual (that is in fact how we're supposed to be treated; that's what we're valued for), you have to be willing to accept the fact that if you are not at least making the cooperative effort, if you are not working on creative projects, creative purposes, then you are not truly human. That's the difference between us and the animal. Yes, you can say we have the potential and we should be treated that way, but the reciprocal side of it is that *you're supposed to think of yourself and act in that way.* Otherwise, if you strip us of that, there isn't that much that distinguishes us biologically, from animals. Every way we are distinguished comes from the fact that we are creative beings. Every thing about our physiology that distinguishes us is tied to the fact that we are cognitive.

For example, speech, language, the ability to do what we do with language, is a cognition driven process. It is driven by the development of human capabilities. *And in a sense, this is the concept of productivity.* We're talking about an increase in the creative, productive powers of labor, which means the ability to discover; it also means the ability to assimilate new knowledge, to act upon it, and without that you don't have a policy. That is why, for example, infrastructure on its own is not itself a solution to the problem. Infrastructure, like a lot of things, can be used a lot of ways. It can be used for good. Conversely, if you're just running military logistics on a highly sophisticated infrastructure, that's not what's needed. That's not going to advance human society. It doesn't increase the productivity of labor.

We're talking about creating a labor force which is like an intellectual labor force. A labor force that organizes itself to assimilate and produce new ideas, not just suggestion box ideas. A labor force which thinks of itself as part of the process of investigating nature, of exploring space. Some object that, "Well, not everybody's involved in the space program," but if you put this together with a real nuclear program and all the infrastructure you need to back up a space program, and all the engineers, and all the schools and all the scientists and all the research facilities, then you realize the entire society is lifted, in terms of its productive capabilities and mission orientation, and indeed the going into space is not just to do an adventure. It is to find out more about the nature of the solar system: How was it created? How do we control the chemical processes? What kind of life is there?

Vladimir Vernadsky, 1911

creative commons

What does it mean if we find other forms of life, even if they're primitive forms of life? What is that going to mean in terms of our ability to develop?

The Fourth Law—Having a 'Certain Vision'

Now if you look at LaRouche's Fourth Law, let me read that section, "Vernadsky on Man and Creation":

V.I. Vernadsky's systemic principle of human nature, is a universal principle, which is uniquely specific to the crucial factor of the existence of the human species. For example: "time" and "space" do not actually exist as a set of metrical principles of the Solar system; their only admissible employment for purposes of communica-

tion is essentially nominal presumption. Since competent science for today can be expressed only in terms of the unique characteristic of the human species' role within the known aspects of the universe, the human principle is the only true principle known to us for practice: the notions of space and time are merely useful imageries.

Now maybe at some point we can get a discussion, it requires some work, to get at what this means. Because, he doesn't necessarily mean, as for example with space travel, "Okay, we have so much space to traverse; we have so many ways to do it, that maybe there is even a time dilation and so on and so forth," Rather, what he is talking about is that there is a quality of space and time that is determined by the human mind—that's determined by the creative nature of the universe itself, that created the solar system. In a certain sense we are traveling in time when we make discoveries; we are discovering where things came from, we are making the past part of the present. All of a sudden, if we know what the past of something is, so to speak, its development, we know a great deal more about what it is now, including why its chemical properties are what they are, how they may have been created, what they may tell us about the processes going on that's a useful part of the solar system. We know there are many, many anomalies in the solar system: the tilt of planets, the nature of the planets, the number of moons, the fact that some of these moons have hot interiors that they are not supposed to have. Where did all this come from?

So the question of space and time are questions of understanding the unique processes of the human mind. And, thereby, that's our access to whatever the creative process in the universe is, whatever people want to call it. In that sense, what we have to bring into the situation is very different, and also means a whole different approach to the development of this planet. We now see for example, in South America, in Africa, nations are saying, "We are going to have nuclear energy." This doesn't just mean they will have nuclear energy plants. It means there are more people who begin to understand what a nuclear process is, how to control radiation, how to use it. It means more potential discoveries, because we are going to have more people working in these areas.

That's what the BRICS [Brazil, Russia, India, China, South Africa] really means. You have to have a certain vision. If we could bring the United States into the world landbridge now, even given as dilapidated as we may be, if you look at this from a somewhat different standpoint, look at it from outside the United States. First of all, look at the lack of conflict. Look at what this may mean to the Russians, the Chinese. Imagine a Big Three with China replacing Great Britain. Now, if that's organized around a real economic development plan, then we have something of tremendous value. And in a sense, that's how we have to look at the Four Laws. Step number one is to get Glass-Steagall, but we have to think of these as four laws. That's up to us. You don't have to always say, "Yes, Glass-Steagall, but that's not enough." The real point is to say Glass-Steagall, *and...* This is why we're doing Glass-Steagall. We're doing Glass-Steagall so we can reinvigorate the space program, increase the productivity of labor. We're going to set up a national bank and credit institutions and so on and so forth for these same purposes.

I think, in some ways, that's why LaRouche invokes Einstein on these matters. But that's the level of thinking that you want. What was Einstein interested in? He was interested in what's the real nature, what's the reality of the universe? What are the actual principles that are operating? How do we get the idea of a single universe? By the way, this is a problem that we still have, and, frankly, after a period where people pooh-poohed this, now at least it is recognized that the ability to incorporate the subatomic world, so-called quantum phenomena, with the questions of gravitational reality, general relativity, special relativity, to bring this together in some concept (not necessarily one mathematical equation): it's a concept of a unified theory of the universe, a unified field. We begin to understand how

EIR

Lyndon H. LaRouche, Jr. at the June 26, 2016 Schiller Institute conference in Berlin.

these things work together.

Every time we discover something, we discover more. For example, one of the differences between Einstein and some of his critics is—their view was the Uncertainty Principle, and I won't go into the details of that now. One version of that is that you can't measure something smaller than the wavelength of the light you use to measure it. The problem is that you are going to hit it with this light that is a lot bigger than it is, and you're going to change its position, change its momentum. Now some of this gets generalized that we're always interfering. And there's some truth to that. We are in the universe, that's the real trick. We're not looking from outside the universe, over the edge of the box, trying to see what's going on. If you look at it that way, yes, we're not really looking at what we think we are looking at. But if you realize we are inside the universe, and you realize that the universe reacts to what you do, and you understand what you are doing, then you have the ability to look over your shoulder and self consciously reflect on the nature of the investigation you are carrying out. And you can find a way to get to that reality. What's the reality of what you have done? And that's Einstein; that's the question Einstein raises.

Striving for Completion

Now LaRouche said, when I was talking to him yesterday, that we are trying, in a certain sense it's our purpose, to get completion. We want to have a completed conception of our institutions, of what they're doing, and we are oriented toward completing our view of the universe, even though it may never be complete. The point is we strive to make it ever more complete. In doing that, that's how the human species survives. We can't exist any other way. The virtue, in one sense, of the classical arts, is that we don't have to wait. You can do classical composition now. You are not going to be able to do the whole solar system now. Frankly, that requires a massive conjoined effort, a common effort of the human species.

The only way you're going to get that is the kind of processes that bring about a new paradigm based on a multiple bringing of other cultures and their classical forms together with ours; that's going to be the basis for the kind of conjoined development that the planet needs. We've seen that somewhat in the organizing here. We know there was something of a metaphysical impact of the concerts [the 9/11 memorial "Requiem" concerts held in New York City in September 2016]. You can't always point to it and say this person was made better, that person was made better... maybe you can in some cases, but the entire situation was made better, not just internally, but in terms of people's relationship to us, and the impact that that had.

You have to think in terms—part of the point LaRouche is making, with the Fourth Law, with his reference to Vernadsky—of what is the actual nature of space and time, and it's not a matter of science fiction, it's not a matter of can we put a guy in some little thing and send him back in time. That's not the question. We can, in fact, use the fact that *cognitive time is different than the time that unfolds in experience*. We can take the time and experience and, from a cognitive standpoint, it can change our understanding of what happens. It can give us powers over the universe that didn't exist up until the point we made those discoveries.

Again it's kind of hard to imagine, in part because there have been so many differences; what was the world like before there was electricity? How much work did you have to do? You lived in the dark. For example, if you lived in this part of the northern hemisphere, you lived in the dark a good deal of the time. Or, think of the following: that the average person, a hundred years ago, even leaving aside the fact that people died at childbirth and so forth, if you were sixty years old, what was your life expectancy? Maybe three or four years. What is your life expectancy today at age sixty? Admittedly it's shrinking, but what is it today, maybe fifteen or twenty years? And obviously with reasonable health care, we can create a potential, where at sixty, your life expectancy is twenty to thirty years. What was it like growing up when you actually realized that you were not likely to make it past forty-five? Take someone like Schiller; yes there were some that made it further, but if you go through the history of great people, an awful lot of them just in the normal course of events didn't make it past fifty-five or sixty—Shakespeare, Beethoven, even FDR. Most of the people in his cabinet were gone between sixty and seventy.

That's a whole change in the situation. That changes time; sometimes not in the best ways. People think they have forever to do something, but that's not the case. You have a certain amount of time to do something, and I think what we have to realize is that the question of the productivity of labor is a *cognitive* question. It is a question of creativity, and that's the nature of human identity, period. There aren't too many of us that are geniuses, admittedly, but at least we are working to make that the way in which the human species acts and gives that opportunity to people in general. That's the identity. It doesn't mean everybody is going to be a whiz kid, but it means that's what you respect, that's what you fight for. That's what you see in other people. And you recognize that this is only done as a joint effort, as cooperation amongst nations.

Remember, LaRouche has been talking about this whole question of finding some basis for a whole different relationship, where sovereignty is important, but is not the final word. This, by the way, was very strong coming out of World War II. MacArthur and many other people thought that because of nuclear weapons, in particular—and FDR having seen World War II—they said we need a different relation among nations. That's why FDR pushed the United Nations, as not a place that overrode national identity, but brought people together to *develop* the planet as a whole from the standpoint of all of these nations. And if anything, that's needed more now than it ever was. But LaRouche's point is that if you are going to do that you have to base it on an appropriate understanding of the nature of mankind. That's in effect what's involved in the fight for these Four Laws.

FOR A NATIONAL SPACE DAY

A Tribute to Astronaut John Glenn, 1921-2016

by Kesha Rogers

As our knowledge of the Universe in which we live increases, may God grant us the wisdom and guidance to use it wisely.

—John Glenn

Dec. 13—I am Kesha Rogers, a former Candidate for U.S. Senate and former Democratic Nominee for the U.S. House of Representatives.

I wish to honor and pay tribute to a great American Hero and Inspiration to the people of this nation, and to many around the world, former Senator and astronaut John Glenn. He died last week, on December 8, 2016.

John Glenn's passing had a profound impact on me, as he died just one day before my 40th birthday. He had been 40 years old when he led the nation to new heights in the conquest of space, being the first American to orbit the Earth, orbiting three times in a nearly five-hour mission. I reflected on his great contributions and his commitment to human progress in the exploration of space. He brought great inspiration to young people around the world and set the nation on a course for the Moon and the opening into space beyond it.

He has gone on to eternally fulfill mankind's extraterrestrial imperative out there somewhere in the Galaxy, or perhaps in some other galaxy. His life was an inspiration to all mankind.

Glenn was one of the chosen seven in the original class of astronauts announced to the world on April 9,

Astronaut John Glenn

NASA

1959; the first to orbit Earth; and the last survivor of the seven. He orbited the Earth three times on February 20, 1962 aboard the *Friendship 7* spacecraft. He was the fifth human in space and the third American. Glenn's mission was truly instrumental in paving the way to achieving the vision of President John F. Kennedy when Kennedy spoke before a joint session of Congress on May 25, 1961 and declared, "I believe this nation should commit itself to achieving the goal, before the decade is out, of landing a man on the Moon and returning him safely to Earth." It was John

Glenn's mission aboard the *Friendship 7* just nine months later that set the nation on course to achieving that goal.

Eight years later, on July 20, 1969, Americans set foot on the surface of the Moon, dedicating their mission to the world with the words, "we came in peace for all mankind."

Although Glenn left his career as an astronaut to serve in the United States Senate for 25 years representing the state of Ohio, beginning in 1974, he never lost his passion for mankind's advance into space. He returned to space in 1998 when he flew in Space Shuttle *Discovery*, the year before he retired from the United States Senate at the age of 77.

Space Launches Development

As we recommit ourselves today to human creative progress, we must restore our national mission for the exploration of space through international cooperation. We must acknowledge mankind's extraterrestrial imperative and recommit ourselves to acting on that principle, to discover and develop the universe. We have a common destiny: All nations must come together to fulfill the mission of developing all mankind.

In an address he gave just a few years ago, astronaut John Glenn prayed that wisdom and guidance be granted by God as mankind's knowledge of the universe increases. He asked, "As our knowledge of the universe in which we live increases, may God grant us the wisdom and guidance to use it wisely."

In his three philosophical laws of astronautics, space pioneer Krafft Ehricke—who would have reached his one hundredth birthday next March—expressed the thought that we are following God's guidance in acting on our extraterrestrial imperative, a necessary expression of mankind's unlimited creative potential in the universe. Ehricke wrote, "By expanding through the universe, man fulfills his destiny as an element of life endowed with the power of reason and the wisdom of the moral law within himself."

Join me in committing this nation to a new system of international relations, a system dedicated to advancing the creative potential of every human being on the planet in order to fulfill mankind's imperative in the exploration of space. We must join with Russia and China in the exploration of space for the peace of all mankind. As the chief engineer of China's manned space program recently declared, "Cooperation between major players will be conducive to the development of all mankind." In a recent white paper issued by China's government that is titled, "The Right to Development: China's Philosophy, Practice and Contribution," the intention to foster human creative progress and increase the productivity of all mankind is clear. The paper begins,

> I call on the United States to declare an annual National Space Day in his memory and the memory of all of the great visionaries of space exploration who have passed the torch and paved the way for a new generation of explorers and discoverers.

Development is a universal human theme, providing for people's basic needs and giving them hope for a better life. The right to development is an inalienable human right, symbolizing dignity and honor ...[1]

Implementing that inalienable human right to develop is truly an imperative of all mankind and starts with a new mission of cooperation in the exploration and development of space. This must be our dedication to the future of humanity, as a spacefaring species.

As we remember and honor astronaut and Senator John Glenn, I call on the United States to declare an annual National Space Day in his memory and the memory of all of the great visionaries of space exploration who have passed the torch and paved the way for a new generation of explorers and discoverers. I call on the United States to establish a new commitment to human development in the exploration of space in cooperation with all nations. Lunar villages and settlements on the Moon will express a shared vision—in a new era of space exploration and international cooperation with Russia and China—of the inalienable right to development of all mankind.

---

1. "The Right to Development: China's Philosophy, Practice and Contribution," issued by the State Council Information Office of the People's Republic of China, December 1, 2016. The full text: http://news.xinhuanet.com/english/china/2016-12/01/c_135873721.htm

www.ingramcontent.com/pod-product-compliance
Lightning Source LLC
Chambersburg PA
CBHW051949280526
45789CB00009B/3222

9 781541 233621